The Synergy Shift

Also by Rev. Shannon E. Karafanda

Until Everyone Hears is the virtual reality home of Shannon's blog and so much more. Visit her at www.UntilEveryoneHears.com.

The Synergy Shift

By
Rev. Shannon E. Karafanda

© 2012 Rev. Shannon E. Karafanda
Published by Room 272 Press
A subsidiary of Anders Peachtree City Properties, LLC
PO Box 2422
Peachtree City, GA 30269
E-mail us at: Shannon@UntilEveryoneHears.com
Visit our website at: www.Room272.weebly.com
Find us on Facebook at www.facebook.com/TheSynergyShift

A portion of the earnings from every book sold by David Anders Publishing House goes to support underprivileged children in our community. Find out more at www.AndersUSA.com.

ISBN-13: 978-0615653532 (Room 272 Press)
ISBN-10: 0615653537

Cover photo: Head Harbour Lightstation, Campobello Island, New Brunswick, Canada. Courtesy Rev. Mark S. Jordan.

Scriptures taken from the Holy Bible,
New International Version®, NIV®.
Copyright © 1973, 1978, 1984 by Biblica, Inc.™
Used by permission of Zondervan. All rights reserved worldwide.
www.zondervan.com
Scripture quotations marked *The Message* are taken from The Message by Eugene Petterson. Copyright © 1993, 1994, 1995, 1996, 2000, 2001, 2002. Used by Permission of NavPress, All Rights Reserved.
Scripture quotations marked GOD'S WORD are taken from GOD'S WORD®, © 1995 God's Word to the Nations. Used by permission of Baker Publishing Group.
Scripture marked NCV is taken from the New Century Version. Copyright © 2005 by Thomas Nelson, Inc. Used by permission. All rights reserved.
Scripture quotations marked (NLT) are taken from the Holy Bible, New Living Translation, copyright © 1996, 2004, 2007 by Tyndale House Foundation. Used by permission of Tyndale House Publishers, Inc., Carol Stream, Illinois 60188. All rights reserved.

All rights reserved. No part of these pages, either text or image may be used for any purpose other than personal use without prior written permission of the holder of the copyright or his legal representative. Therefore, reproduction, modification, storage in a retrieval system or retransmission, in any form or by any means, electronic, mechanical or otherwise, for reasons other than personal use, is strictly prohibited without prior written permission of the holder of the copyright or his legal representative. LEB. The views expressed in this work are solely those of the author and do not necessarily reflect the views of the publisher, and the publisher hereby disclaims any responsibility for them.

Table of Contents

Foreword: i

Chapter 1: This Was My Time 1

Chapter 2: The Roller Coaster 15

Chapter 3: Weird-Ass Issues 23

Chapter 4: The Big Ask 27

Chapter 5: Organizational Systems 31

Chapter 6: Unbalanced 33

Chapter 7: Drugs and Disney 35

Chapter 8: Saying Good-Bye 41

Chapter 9: First Impressions 47

Chapter 10: Answering Your Own Questions 53

Chapter 11: The Holy Spirit—A Hostage Situation 57

Chapter 12: Game On! 61

Chapter 13: Superheroes 65

Chapter 14: The Duck 69

Chapter 15: 'Ohana Means Family 73

Chapter 16: Celebrations 77

Notes: 82

Study Guide for Group Discussions: 84

This book is dedicated to Linda Freeman, my 6th grade English teacher, who wrote in my yearbook, "One day I expect to see your name in print." And to teachers, youth pastors, counselors, and mentors everywhere who help young people realize and discover their dreams.

Foreword

A lighthouse is a beautiful thing. In most cases, a lighthouse stands majestically on the horizon of a picturesque scene. My mother's side of the family comes from coastal Canada, so I have had the opportunity on a number of occasions to visit some of the most famous lighthouses in the world. To stand at the base of one and look to the light is an amazing experience, and one that has humbled me on a number of occasions. I love a lighthouse.

When one thinks about lighthouses, however, it is important to know that they are not built for postcards and picturesque scenery. Though they certainly are beautiful, they were not created purely for the sake of being beautiful... they have a definitive purpose and role to play. You see, lighthouses exist for the storm. Lighthouses exist for the fog. Lighthouses exist for the darkness. Lighthouses exist to be a beacon of light and hope in the midst of nature's calamity, to enable seafarers to navigate treacherous landscapes and all that nature can throw their way.

When I first read the book, *The Synergy Shift*, I could not help but think about the purpose of a lighthouse and the church known as Lighthouse in Shannon Karafanda's life experience. The beautiful thing to know, though, is Lighthouse is not only powerfully poignant for Shannon's life, but for the lives of many others. I know this to be true, because it is true for me. The stories contained in these pages are evidence of God's amazing grace through the trials and tribulations of life. It can often be hard to recognize God's hand at work in the midst of life's storms, but the fact of the matter is that one's personal story has the ability to point us to a greater truth... God's truth! This book certainly did that for me. You see, in many ways, the stories in these pages are also my story. And since all stories of truth point to the ultimate Source of Truth – Jesus Christ – these stories are now part of God's story and absolutely must be told.

It is with great joy that I recommend this book to you. There are stories that will make you laugh and stories that will make you cry. There is powerful evidence of the Hand of God upon a situation that on the surface seemed hopeless at best. Through it all, however, the love of God shined and shines still as a way to remind us that no matter how ferociously the storm may rage, how dense the fog may be, or how dark the night might fall, we are never too far away to be found by the light and love of God through Jesus Christ! Whether your storm is in your work, your family, your church, or wherever, may you be inspired to follow the vision for life (AND ministry!) as given by God.

The Apostle Paul wrote in 2 Corinthians 4.6: "For God, who said, 'Let light shine out of darkness,' made his light shine in our hearts to give us the light of the knowledge of God's glory displayed in the face of Christ." May you be blessed to know that your story matters as a way to convey the power of hope and love to people who need it. As Shannon Karafanda has so eloquently and honestly shared her story, may you also heed the challenging call to share yours as well. You have no idea just how important it might be for someone weathering a storm or fumbling in the darkness to see how God has worked in your life. It might be more than a lighthouse, it might be a lifesaver. May this wonderful book, *The Synergy Shift*, be of help to you on your own spiritual journey!

Rev. Dr. Mark S. Jordan
Pastor and Director
The Lighthouse Ministries
Sharpsburg, Georgia

Chapter 1: This Was My Time

syn·er·gy

[**sin**-er-jee]
noun, plural syn·er·gies.
    The interaction of elements that when combined produce a total effect that is greater than the sum of the individual elements, contributions, etc.; synergism

    God is weird. Just when I think I get it, He surprises me with something that turns my world upside down. On August 3, 2006 my best friend died. That alone can turn anyone's world into chaos. But you see, this was no ordinary best friend. This was Allan Todd. Okay, I know that name sounds pretty ordinary but let me assure you, he was not. I guess at first glance he looked like your typical overweight American dude: middle class, two kids, great family. But Allan was definitely different: larger than life, full of spirit, called to greatness—the type of person who will change your life.

    Before I go on to tell you how saintly he was, let me assure you he had his faults. But those little things that annoy you when someone is around you seem forgotten when you'll never see them again. The moment he died, my life seemed so foreign to me. There was a hole in my heart that ached to be filled. Time before and after Allan's death was segmented into separate moments, and it all happened in a matter of minutes.

    What made Allan different wasn't who he was per se but what we were doing. We had been meeting for about a year with several other people to start a new church named Lighthouse—a different kind of church. A church that we believed was what God really wanted us to offer to the people of Fayette County, Georgia. Our focus was on innovative, contemporary worship and frequent service projects in our local area. This may not sound too radical to some, but the reality is that most churches don't focus on these things. Many are country clubs. Some are country clubs to which no one wants to belong. We planned to be different and exciting.

Allan died about a week before our Grand Opening. We had everything ready. We were so excited—and then I got the phone call that changed my life.

One of Lighthouse's members, Jennifer Ellison, called me while I was making dinner. My family had just gotten back from *Meet the Teacher Day* at the kids' elementary school and my boys were excited about their classrooms and friends. My husband John was walking through the door, coming home from work. The pasta was boiling on the stove. These mundane details stick in my mind to add normalcy to an event that was so devastating and still often surreal to me.

Jennifer told me that Abby, Allan's oldest daughter, had called her to let her know that they couldn't bring dinner to her. I guess Allan had made a meal (like he always did to show hospitality) since Jennifer's family was moving into a new house. Abby told her that Allan had been taken to the hospital but she didn't say much more. Abby and her sister Hannah were at their neighbor's house and seemed pretty upset. But even in the middle of all that Abby kept apologizing about the meal. Jennifer wanted to know if I knew anything.

I reassured her that it was probably nothing. He'd been recovering from pneumonia. It was probably just related to that. I thanked her for calling me because Allan wasn't the type to talk about his health and I'd probably find out tomorrow and he'd blow it off.

I finished cooking dinner. I ate with the boys but worried the whole time. After dinner I tried to find his wife's cell number. At the time, Pam (Allan's wife) and Allan rarely used their cell phones so all I had was a home number for her. I was about to call the hospital when she called me. She said she thought that Allan had a heart attack. He was taken away in an ambulance and she was just getting to the hospital and was going back to see him. I asked if she needed me there. She cried and said that she just didn't want to be alone.

I rushed to the hospital and a thousand things went through my mind. I tried to call our band leader to tell him that Allan wouldn't be at practice and to ask the band to pray for him. I got his voicemail. I thought about the opening worship service and what would happen. I thought Allan might have surgery or at least have to recover for a while. Would I preach? Would we postpone?

I came in the ER doors and asked to see Allan Todd. They asked my name and someone came back to take me to Pam. She was crying but very clearly said, "He didn't make it."

I must have said, "What?" because she said, "He died."

She collapsed on me and we both cried. At least I think I cried. I was in such disbelief I couldn't really feel anything for a few minutes. Pam kept saying, "But we've got a church to start!"—over and over. She explained to everyone in the room about Lighthouse. No one starts a church alone. At the very least they have their family. Pam was just as invested as Allan and his death had a ripple effect that went through their family, my family, and so many others.

Then someone came back and told us that Allan's body was ready for Pam to see. I followed her back and saw him lying on the table. I kept expecting him to jump up and say *Boo!* and laugh while I peed in my pants. But he was gone, really gone.

Pam hugged all over him and cried. She kept looking back at me and asking, "What are we going to do?"

I had no answer. The planner and organizer in me wanted to tell her step by step what was going to happen. I think I even attempted that once or twice. All I could do was be there for her and, even then, I still felt helpless.

I experienced every emotion that night. I guess remembering someone so close to you can do that. I never got mad at God and I never asked *why?* Doing so seemed pointless. I do remember thinking *what now?*

Dead bodies have always freaked me out. It gives me the heebie jeebies to realize that just a short time ago a body could move and now it can't. The body looks the same, yet really doesn't. Part of the problem could have been the lack of funerals that I went to as a child. Between the ages of zero and eighteen I went to a total of two funerals. And both of those were closed casket.

So when I was called into the ministry, I knew that this could be an issue for me. After all, if I were to officiate a funeral I might actually have to be near and maybe even see a dead body. I thought about only saying yes to funerals where cremation was involved but this seemed a bit impractical.

I was hoping that I'd get the opportunity to actually get up the nerve to see and perhaps touch a dead body before my first funeral. I know that sounds odd. Who has this as a hope for the betterment of his or her career? I had a few opportunities but the best chance I had was to see the open casket across the room. And then the request came for my first funeral.

It was for a six month old baby named Jenny. The story was that she fell when she was being changed. I got called in as 3rd string to do the funeral because the Senior Pastor and another pastor friend of the family were all out of town. Can you image the shell shock? Here was my first funeral; this was their first child; and I was discussing funeral arrangements. It just didn't seem right at all. I hadn't met anyone from the family but the grandmother before the funeral (and I'd only met her once).

Although Jenny did not suffer any visual, physical damage, the family opted to have a closed casket during visitation. The immediate family did, however, meet at the funeral home before processing to the church for the funeral. It was there that they had an open casket. Just before they put her in the hearse, I went back to see her. She looked literally like a doll. Just beautiful and precious as if she had no cares in the world. I'd only seen one picture of her with her eyes open but I could tell that this wasn't really the same girl. This was an image that the funeral home was able to create. I knew where the real Jenny was. She was with Jesus. She wasn't here anymore.

The day she died that family lost a lot of dreams. Dreams for what Jenny would do as she grew up. Dreams for a family. Dreams for a lifetime. When Allan died dreams were lost too. Dreams for a church. Dreams for his family. Dreams for many lifetimes.

In both cases new dreams were created. Hope through a new baby girl. A church that went on to thrive. A family that was still able to find love.

As of this writing, Allan was the last dead body I've seen. A dead body is very different before a funeral home gets its hands on it. Allan was lying on a hospital table with a tube still taped to his cheek. He was just minutes past his last breath. For just those few moments, my life was not real. I still think back to it and feel the cloud of haze that surrounded my thoughts during that time. Allan was with Jesus, too.

I'll never forget the sight of both Jenny and Allan after they passed away. Those images are burned in my head forever. My heart aches thinking about each lying so still. All of the dreams shattered. All of the life gone.

The only thing that gets me out of the hurt, out of the funk and moving on is that I know that even though their life is gone from here, it continues elsewhere. Their lives, although cut short, remind us of how precious life is. Life is a gift. Against all odds, two people came together to create a special and unique DNA that is me or you or Allan or Jenny. I would give anything to be able to talk to Allan right now. And I would have really liked to have held Jenny and rocked her as a baby. But I feel blessed to have known both of them the ways that I did—even if it wasn't long enough.

After Pam had said her goodbyes, I drove her home so she could tell her girls, Abby and Hannah. The plan was for her to pick them up from next door and I would lag behind and tell the neighbors. That plan went out the window the moment they saw me and Pam. They demanded to know what happened. Pam said, "He didn't make it." Then I heard the most horrible sound I've ever heard in my life. It was the sound of Abby and Hannah's hearts breaking. They were twelve and ten years old at the time. Their sobs pierced my heart and I immediately began the ugly cry – sobbing without sound and not certain if I could stop.

We got the girls home and talked a bit. I made a few phone calls but I wasn't sure if people believed me. I wasn't even sure I believed it yet. How do you say something like that over the phone?

Within minutes people started arriving. Most wore the same stunned expression that I was feeling. Some sobbed. Many hugged. The night dragged on and on as we called people and others started popping in.

With all of the people around who loved Allan and worshiped at Lighthouse, I never felt so close to God, and at the same time, so isolated from the rest of the world. I didn't sleep much that night; maybe an hour. I cried myself to sleep, then got up before sunrise and prepared for my saddest day of work ever. Until that day, I had the best job ever. It wasn't great just because of the work I did. It was fun because of who I worked with. Allan made it fun because of what we shared and the relationship we had built.

In the few decades that men and women have come to work more closely in the workplace, a new phenomenon has occurred – the relationship of the *office spouse*. An office spouse is one who knows what buttons to push, what makes his or her co-worker angry or happy, where he or she likes to eat for lunch, and when he or she will be leaving on a Friday before a long weekend. An office spouse can also tell you honestly when you're being a *big-itch* and can also share deep feelings in a totally platonic way.

After working at Lighthouse with Allan for a few weeks, we discovered something strange. We could finish each other's sentences. We could also read each other's minds with just a look. We had become very quickly *office spouses*. It is a strange and wonderful thing to have an office spouse. My husband is a wonderful person and I love him dearly but he couldn't tell you the difference between eschatology and soteriology even if he were in a theological library and had a team of professors at his disposal. It's not that he's stupid, he's actually quite smart. It's just that he doesn't care. He loves me and he supports what I do but he really doesn't care to do it himself. And although he would gladly listen if I needed to talk, he really doesn't want to hear theological ideas or church political discussions after he comes home from a day of Systems Analysis and Design. And even in those times that he does engage me in a theological discussion, we'll sometimes end up disagreeing and I'll get more upset with him than I would a Jehovah's Witness on a Saturday morning.

But when you have an office spouse, things are different. You can vent about the job with a person who understands and has an interest—someone who has an educated guess as to what to do instead of a personal opinion.

Allan was a big fan of *The West Wing*. He loved the intrigue and suspense on the show. Allan knew early on that if he were going to be starting this church, he needed a *Leo*—the Chief of Staff who kept things running. He made the President look good. Allan's gift was with people. He could dream big dreams and after meeting with someone for just a few minutes have them dreaming the same dream and working on a plan to get there.

Allan was *not* an administrator. He couldn't type and needed someone to check his emails, voicemails, and calendar. It wasn't that he felt too proud to do these things, he really couldn't keep up with them. His organizational style consisted of yellow legal pads. He kept a different yellow legal pad for every meeting, every sermon, and every idea. And when he went to file these away he might put an office meeting under *office* and the next time put it under *administration* and the next time under *organizational meeting*. Allan needed me (or someone) to keep him on track. I became his Leo.

In that first week after his death, I couldn't imagine a world without Allan in it. What function would I have without him to support? Who was the Chief of Staff without his or her President to support? What was going to happen now?

I can't remember now if I actually ever told him how much fun working at Lighthouse had been. I LOVED going to work every day. It was never a job; it was an adventure.

The day after his death was different. That day I hated being in the office. I felt lost and definitely alone. For the most part I just sat there and cried. I called our marketing contact at the local radio station and told him to hold off on the radio advertisements. I told him to pray. I called the band playing at our opening celebration and told them there might be a change in plans. Then I told them to pray. I sent out an email to my closest friends and told them my heart was breaking and asked them to pray. The only prayer that I could lift up was *Oh God, Oh God, Oh God*. In fact, I'm not sure if I said anything else for the first two hours that I was there.

One of our congregants brought me doughnuts. The funny thing is that for the first time in my life I couldn't eat a doughnut. I had expected to binge-eat for the next few days, but I couldn't eat much of anything.

At some point I felt the prayers start working and I began to get phone calls of support and sympathy. I guess I really was Allan's office spouse because people were realizing my loss even amid their own despair.

At some point my thoughts began to focus on Lighthouse.

What was going to happen? The Director of New Church Development for the North Georgia United Methodist Church, Parks Davis, called and said he'd like to speak with the leadership of the church. He thought that the launch should go on. My first question was – with whom? What role would I play? How would the leaders at the UMC know who would be a good fit for us?

Later in the day, many people showed up to cry and be comforted. Parks stopped by to get a feel for what was happening. I was so happy when someone suggested that I become Senior Pastor. There was something comforting about not having a stranger lead us. Of course Parks, not knowing me from a hole in the wall, began to back-pedal. He probably squirmed a bit in a humorous sort of way, trying not to step on anyone's toes. I tried to convince him that I was up for the challenge which might also have seemed funny since I was blubbering as I said it. Who would put faith in someone like that?

Of course given my feelings for Allan and for Lighthouse, his response, although pastoral, was painful. I frankly don't remember him saying anything, but the silence that followed, as he pondered what to say, spoke loudly. He saw that I was hurting and had a hard time imagining me in any other role at the moment. I just couldn't imagine someone else here. No one could be Allan Todd. No team would ever be like the two of us. And the realization that I'd lost more than a friend seemed to ache in every part of me.

Okay, I would have never stroked Allan's ego when he was here in front of me, but I really did miss his wisdom. How many times did he have really important things to say that seemed like simple, common sense but really helped me be a better person, leader, minister?

Later that night I was told that our District Superintendent (DS) was going to preach at our Grand Opening. She's a talented, faithful person, but I felt like I was getting pushed further away from what was once familiar and my shock and denial quickly turned to anger. I kept thinking like a spoiled child and drawing imaginary mental lines in the sand.

If the Conference won't let me preach or puts someone here who doesn't honor the vision, then I'm starting a new church at my house! Non-denominational!

At least that's how I felt before I spoke with Allan's best friend, Bert McDade. I finally saw where Allan's wisdom came from – and Allan was passing Bert's wisdom off as his own! Bert told me one of the names mentioned to be appointed at Lighthouse and for some reason that didn't make me mad. It actually gave me peace. If Lighthouse couldn't accept a new pastor then could we really accept new members as we grow? How could I do this without a team? Bert calmed me down a bit. He stroked my ego by telling me how important I was to Lighthouse's future – regardless of my title. I did not like hearing it at first, but after it sunk in it helped me out.

Then I talked to my mentor, Rev. Betsy Haas. She had been an Associate Pastor for many years, so she was able to sympathize from a different angle. I told her my reasons for wanting to take over the church and the world and wanting to make sure the vision kept going. She told me that I was called to be #2 at Lighthouse and that I needed to do that at my best until I truly felt called to be #1. She was a great listening ear for me.

The Sunday after Allan's death was actually quite beautiful. God was there. People's lives were changed. But from my point of view it all SUCKED!! During the morning worship service, I welcomed people and shared what had happened. I don't know how I said what I did. The words just came out. I told everyone that while Allan was on his way to do an act of hospitality and service, he passed away. Fitting that he was serving others as he died.

We showed the video *This is Your Time,* by Michael W. Smith, which had been our theme for the summer. It made me cry even more. Bert preached about the disciples after Jesus died. I bet Allan *loved* being compared to Jesus! That's okay, I loved being compared to the disciples, so I guess we all have egos. Bert was really funny! I don't know how he did all that knowing he had lost Allan, and would be preaching at the funeral later that same day. He was great.

At the end, people came forward to get hour glasses that we'd ordered to symbolize that this was *our time*. Bert asked them to come forward and get them from me as a sign that they were still committed to the vision. Everyone came forward and I told each one that they were created *for such a time as this.* (Esther 4:14 NIV)

Before the service, I told Parks that I wanted a team back so that I didn't have to go through starting this new church alone. I understood that I'd been staying under the radar, but I told him I trusted him and the Cabinet (the group of pastors who provide oversight and direction for particular areas of the United Methodist Church). I don't know if I did, but I really didn't trust myself at that moment and I needed to mourn and not worry so much about Lighthouse's future with all of that pressure on me.

Then the funeral came. There were 1,000 people there. It was a great tribute to Allan's dedication and commitment to follow his call into servant leadership in the church. Four people spoke, each giving funny and sentimental stories about memories that showed Allan's passion for life and love.

After the service, I met someone unexpected—Allan's middle school friend who had invited Allan on his first youth retreat. Several times, Allan told the story of this friend who invited him on a retreat and, from that moment on, Allan started going to church and later brought his parents. Before that retreat, Allan's family had been through turmoil as his sister chose the wrong path and eventually took her own life. Allan always used this story to encourage us to invite someone to a church event because you never know when that invitation will change someone's life. I told Allan's friend that he was responsible for all of the people in the room whose lives had been changed by Allan Todd. I asked him to look around. I told him that if he'd never invited Allan to church, then none of those people would have the relationship with God that they do. You often hear of how one little thing can change the world. His small invitation did. I thanked him. I can't even remember his name but, if it weren't for him, the emptiness I felt at that moment would be a way of life instead of a moment of sorrow.

As we progressed through the week of the launch, I felt like I was in a war zone. There was so much to do. This kind of stuff was Allan's strength. I can get a sermon ready or put together a Vacation Bible School but the details of a big event like this, where so much is on the line, stressed me out. I put large poster sheets of paper around the room with all of the things we needed to do. I'm a visual person and this seemed like the best plan of attack. Tuesday night we had a meeting and all of our heavy hitters showed up to volunteer. We gave everyone a job to do. We got all places filled. We had a hospitality plan and a follow up plan.

The District Superintendent came by to see how things were going and to tell me that I should preach the opening. I felt relieved and yet I didn't know how I could convince people to join a new church where the pastor just died. I really needed someone to talk to who understood what it meant to move forward with this kind of vision. I felt like Allan was the only one who would understand. He was my rock. He was the ear I needed. That week seemed very lonely. The office was so very quiet. I kept expecting him to walk through the door. Little things like changing his voicemail and looking at his office desk were such enormous tasks. How could I delete his voice when I wanted to hear it every day? But how could I leave his voice there when the church had to move on in his absence?

I kept thinking each night that I'd wake up and this hole in my heart would be filled. I asked God to fill it, but He just surrounded it. He told me that I really shouldn't fill it; that I needed to work with it and use my pain to change the world. Well, it certainly changed mine. It hurt so much. I never realized what a fun and exciting, alive person I was until I started walking through this fog of uncertainty that seemed as if it would never lift.

On launch day, I prayed like never before. Only the Holy Spirit could see me through this. Allan always prayed with the band and some key leaders before each service. Before every prayer he said, "Today we'll have somewhere between 5 and 500 people, but someone today will hear about God's love in a new and powerful way, possibly for the first time."

That day I was nervous, but also confident that the people would come. Allan and I had a mock bet on how many people would be at our opening. He kept praying for 250. I kept praying for 500 and told him that since my faith was stronger, I knew I'd win. Of course, after what had happened, I knew we would have a lot of sympathy supporters, but it was still amazing to peek at the crowd knowing that we were going to fill so much of the auditorium.

I went up to pray with the band. I told them, "Guys, it's more than five. Someone will experience God today for the first time, and we will experience God today in a new way. God is with us. Allan is with us. And in the moment before we start, they both are proud!"

The music was amazing, the energy was intense and I felt a pure form of worship. Everyone was there for God, relying on God for strength, for hope, for support.

If you look at scripture, you'll see that God is a God of numbers. Jesus fed the 5000. Peter converted 3000 at Pentecost. Revelation is full of numbers, but it doesn't really matter if you have five or 500. What matters is that God is there for the five just as much as for 500. When God works in the lives of the five, great things begin to happen and before you know it 500 more people are affected. So your numbers might be big during one worship service, but they could also be big just by sending out twelve ordinary people to change the world. That day we had 367.

For my sermon I used the only hint that Allan had given me about his sermon topic on that day. I used the idea of a blank canvas. I reminded everyone that for a year we had been asking *what if* questions. What if we had a church focused on others and not ourselves? What if we did service projects often and locally? What if we grew through small group studies in our homes? What if hospitality was hugely important to us? What if what others got out of worship was more important for us than what we got out of it? What if we were committed to God, our family, and our church in that order? This church was new. It was a blank canvas and the way that we would fill our canvas is by reaching out to people who needed God the most. I asked everyone there to think of someone who could benefit from a church like this and if they were so led, to come to the altar and write their friend's name or initials on blank canvases that we had set up. During our prayer time, so many people came down that our canvases were full.

In that moment, it didn't matter that Allan had died. What mattered was that the vision was God's and now instead of just thinking about it, we could see it, too. We could see the vision being lived out. The vision was now ours.

I know I'll look back on that day a million times and wonder how it would have been if Allan were there. If he had been at the opening, how many people would have attended and who would have become a part of the Lighthouse dream? But in that moment I felt that even though Allan died, at least this part of him that was greater than him, lived on as a church, in his family and in all of our hearts. Life goes on even after death. He just changed locations.

Allan, I love you. I don't think I told you this when you were with me. There was a very clear call for me to know you and for me to be a part of Lighthouse with you. And I now know that I was created *for such a time as this.*

For if you remain silent at this time, relief and deliverance for us will arise from another place, but you and your family will perish. And who knows but that you have come to your position for such a time as this?
—Esther 4:11, paraphrased NIV

Chapter 2: The Roller Coaster

syn·er·gy
  [**sin**-er-jee]
***noun, plural* syn·er·gies.**
> Physiology, Medicine/Medical. The cooperative action of two or more muscles, nerves or the like

Allan used to tell the story of his infamous date at the county fair. He and his buddy had a double date and they were taking the girls for a night of rides and games. Allan had incredibly bad motion sickness and would turn the worst shade of green at the thought of riding a roller coaster. So he and his friend worked out a deal. They were going to try and stick to the carnival games and Ferris wheel. If the girls suggested that they wanted to ride a roller coaster, they'd start to get in line but once they got there, if the ride looked too bumpy to Allan, he'd say, "Hey, aren't you getting hungry?" and the buddy was supposed to say "yes" and step out to join Allan in getting a snack for everyone. This way the girls had an even number to ride with but Allan didn't look like a wimp.

Unfortunately for Allan, when they got to the fair, of course, the girls wanted to go on the roller coaster. So Allan (as planned) got up to the line and said, "Hey don't you want to get something to eat?" and his buddy said "Nah" and they walked right up and got on—all four of them. Allan threw up on his date and spent the rest of the night trying to recover.

Ministry is like a roller coaster. Sometimes it can be a thrill a minute. Sometimes it seems all uphill and you can't see what's on the other side. Sometimes you go downhill so fast you think you just might crash. And sometimes even the thought of another day can make you a bit queasy.

I vaguely remember riding my first roller coaster. I was about five years old and went on a field trip to Six Flags over Georgia with the summer day camp I was attending. I remember that we had to hold onto the stupid boating rope as we walked through the park. At the time, I'm sure it gave me comfort that if I held onto the rope I wouldn't get lost. Now I'm embarrassed for the little girl who was paraded about with her classmates because we were too immature to walk on our own.

At Six Flags there are a few roller coasters that you don't have to be too tall to ride. The Great American Scream Machine is one of these. It is an old wooden roller coaster that drops nearly 90 feet, reaches a speed of 57 mph and lasts about two minutes. To a five year old, the ride drops the same height as a sky scraper, reaches speeds of a rocket ship, and lasts about thirty minutes. I have no idea why they let me on the ride. I really think it was even crazier to let a whole class of kindergarteners who couldn't even walk in a straight line without a rope on the ride.

There are some kids who are thrill seekers from the womb, but when it comes to G forces, I'm not one of them. I spent the entire ride letting this roller coaster live up to its name. My teacher in the car in front of me heard my panicked screams, and reached behind her to hold onto me the entire ride. Just the feel of her hand on mine, was enough to anchor me to safety. I got off that ride and did not ride another roller coaster until I was in college.

In many ways my faith journey took a similar turn. My parents were involved in a Methodist church before I was born. They worked with the youth group and were close with the pastor and his family since they were near the same age. I don't have many memories of what church was like when I was young, but I do remember that most of the activities for kids three and under were for the enjoyment of the parents and congregation, and not for the toddlers. We were paraded around the church every so often (usually without a rope) and asked to stand still as long as possible on the *stage* (aka near the pulpit) in our Sunday best so that the adults could gawk at us. Now that I have children of my own, I totally understand the gawking. There is a spiritual blessing at being able to gawk at cute children and to know that they will someday keep the church going, but when I was three years old, all I saw was a room full of faces and the image was terrifying.

At some point, my parents discovered that the thrill of church involvement could be crushed by the dark side of church politics and we left and stayed away until I was in high school. Sometimes all it takes is one bad experience like this for people to turn away from a relationship with God. The church is often its own worst enemy when it comes to reaching people for the transformation of the world.

Conversely, Allan's family had one bad experience outside the church that brought them to a closer relationship with God. Allan's sister committed suicide when she was in her early twenties. I believe she had been suffering from drug addiction, but it was something Allan didn't speak of often so I don't have the whole story. I do know that because of this situation his heart was searching for something and he grew closer to God.

It was because of our own personal situations that we had a heart for people who were searching. I was hoping to create a church where people who had been *hurt* by church could find their faith again, and Allan was hoping to create a church where people could have their *hurt* healed. It wouldn't be easy but it would be a thrilling ride.

So back to the roller coaster…

Roller coasters have no engines. Instead, the car is pulled to the top of the first hill and released, then it rolls freely along the track without any external mechanical assistance for the remainder of the ride. The law of conservation of energy states that energy can neither be created nor destroyed, thus, the purpose of the ascent of the first hill is to build up potential energy that will then be converted to kinetic energy as the ride continues. The initial hill, or the lift hill, is the tallest in the entire ride. As the train is pulled to the top, it gains potential energy.

This process of converting kinetic energy to potential energy and back to kinetic energy continues with each hill. The energy is never destroyed, but is lost to friction between the car and track. Brakes finally bring the ride to a complete stop.

This makes sense to me. You build up potential energy and then let it go. The beginning of the ride builds anticipation and the remainder of the ride is thrilling. Why then is there such a problem with starting and growing a church? There should be a clear start, a building of momentum and then some great times enjoying the ride. But as most church planters could tell you, it doesn't always work that way. To someone like me who graduated with a management degree from an engineering school, it is very frustrating that I can't manage everyone into telling me the technicalities of an answer.

Then one day a light bulb went off in the dark corners of my mind. I'd been tutoring a local high school student who was failing Algebra II in a big bad way. I told her I could help. You know because pastors use Algebra and Trig on a daily basis so it should be no problem right? Actually it wasn't too hard. I was a math geek in high school so I remembered more than I thought and was able to look up the rest. I'll also brag a bit here —she pulled her final grade up to a B.

I really didn't teach her much math, rather some study skills she was lacking. Her school teacher was new to teaching after having been an engineer for twenty years or so. His teaching style was different than what my friend was used to but not all that different from what she'd encounter in college. I just taught her how to study a different way and what questions she needed to ask. I hope that those lessons stick more than her memory of the Unit Circle.

For her final exam, we were reviewing the graphing of inequalities. Basically it is just like graphing a regular line except that you need to shade certain parts of the graph to show it could be > or < and/or = any point on said line. For those of you who can't picture the visual it all boils down to there not being just one answer for the problem. There are several points that answer the equation and several that don't. Separating the two is the goal.

Which brings me back to my light bulb moment... God is not linear.

Being the math geek that I am, I constantly want to put God in my list of bulleted things to do and/or understand. I want to get to the next level of Christianity by doing x, y, and z; but, as I'm reminded, God is not linear and as I'm created in God's image, neither am I.

There are a lot of things that God is NOT. God is not evil, stupid, or apathetic. There are a lot of things I'm not. I am not boring, tall, or fashionable. There are a lot of things that God is. God is gracious, loving, and strong. I am insightful, funny, and driven. But even with all of these things that I am and am not and the things that God is and is not, there are a whole host of things we can't even begin to fathom. If God were linear, then we would know all points on the line. We would understand EXACTLY who God is. And so my friends,

I'm happy to say that God is not linear. God is *greater than* what we can imagine. And that makes our journey even more exciting.

As a former programmer and continual geek, I tend to think in processes and if/then statements. If potential member X visits our church, then X will want to serve in position A. If potential member Y visits our church, then neighbors Q, T, and Z will visit as well eventually ending in a 10% increase in membership. Annoying, huh?

It's just who I am. I can't change it so I must learn to use it for good. One such process that has always fascinated me is the infinite loop. Usually programmers don't realize they've put these in until they crash the entire system or cannot get their new code to complete. An infinite loop is basically a set of instructions in a computer program which loops endlessly, either due to the loop having no terminating condition, having one that can never be met, or one that causes the loop to start over.

A simple example of this is

```
int x = 0;
while (x < 10)
println(x);
x = x — 1;
```

In this case X will ALWAYS be less than 10, so the process will continue looping forever. It doesn't really matter if you understand this. What matters is that you can recognize if you are caught in one and what action to take at that point.

I have discovered that the church is a place of infinite loops as well. Some good some bad. Here are a few of those examples:

1) The *We've Always Done It That Way* Loop, also known as the *Tradition With No Purpose* Loop. At some point someone did something and someone else thought it was good and therefore, it became tradition. Traditions can be good. Spending time together at Christmas is a great tradition and one that I'm not likely to break. But tradition with no purpose can get out of control and really hard to break. I served at a church once that had a Bible on the Altar that was too large for the table. On days when we served communion it was

very difficult to place the elements on the altar. When I suggested that we substitute one of the smaller, historical church Bibles that were on display in the hallway, I was dismissed with a *we've always had that one* remark. Side note—the church was 150 years old and the Bible was only 40 years old, but I digress. This really didn't bother me too much until one day I was flipping through said Bible to find a scripture passage and noticed that there were many pages missing from this Bible—3.5 books of the Bible to be exact. And thus the example of the infinite loop that needs some de-bugging.

2) The *We've Got To Help Them* Loop—Helping others should never be a loop without an escape condition. The purpose of helping others is to get them back on their feet so that they can be the people God created them to be. If we help them to relieve the situation but don't help the cause, we are creating an infinite loop where a person could possibly become dependent on our help. If you want to really see this in action, volunteer to answer your church's phone for one day. It's amazing how many calls you'll get from people needing bills paid or food handouts. It is sad really that there are so many people who need help and have no one else to call. Please understand, I'm all for helping people. But there are ways to help others in the short term and ways to help them long term. The key is to find out how to balance both.

3) The *Infinite God* Loop—This is the good loop and the one you want to be a part of. The one that never ends and will keep on going and going and going. I like that my beliefs are part of a *Kingdom that has no end*. And when I'm part of a process that focuses on this infinite loop of love, I can feel, experience, and see that Kingdom now. Don't try to hack into this one. There are too many firewalls. Your name is your username and your password is belief. That is all you need.

Sorry for the bad puns, but like I said, I am who I am and I'm learning to deal with it!

Getting caught in this loop requires getting on the ride. You may get caught in a loop you don't want to be in but should get to meet some great people and, hopefully, be able to see some great miracles and transformations in the process.

When Allan and I took some students to Universal Studios the summer before we launched Lighthouse, he was still too chicken to go on the rides. He went to all the shows and became the official *bag watcher* for the kids. At some point I tried to convince him to go on the Spider-man ride. As we waited to go on the ride, we were able to see some previews of the ride on TVs in the waiting area. The more we stood there the more he realized that this ride would have a few too many turns and dips for his stomach to handle. When we got to the point to get on, he told the person working the ride that he was going to let me go ahead and he'd wait for me at the end. I rode the ride alone and enjoyed the thrill knowing that Allan was better off not throwing up on me.

Allan never got to see the finished product of what God had called him to. I often wonder why he never got to finish the ride but then maybe he did. He stayed faithful the entire time and for God that is more than enough.

Then the LORD said to him, "This is the land I promised on oath to Abraham, Isaac and Jacob when I said, 'I will give it to your descendants.' I have let you see it with your eyes, but you will not cross over into it."
—*Deuteronomy 34:4, NIV*

Chapter 3: Weird-Ass Issues

Synergy is the highest activity of life; it creates new untapped alternatives; it values and exploits the mental, emotional, and psychological differences between people.
—*Stephen Covey*

The world is full of Granola – fruits, flakes, and nuts. And the church is not immune. In fact, sometimes, on rare occasions of course, a church can be a breeding ground for these people. Sadly these few nutty people often give the universal Church a bad name.

Even in ministry, we can see our share of Granola that become ordained clergy. Not in my denomination, but I've heard stories elsewhere. Where I went to seminary, Emory University's Candler School of Theology, we had some of the best and brightest. We also had some of the fruitiest and nuttiest. Many of the nuts, I'm sorry to say, were women. I never once had a class that didn't have a woman that had a chip on her shoulder and was out to prove that women were superior and all men were out to get them. These women comprised only a small percentage of the total women there, but they were loud, abrasive, and often abusive. Some of these women have even been ordained in various denominations and now women in ministry may have a reputation with some as having – you guessed it – weird-ass issues.

I know that everybody has their issues. Everybody's been hurt, done something stupid, has some sort of phobia or compulsive behavior that is not the norm. However, people may cross boundaries and allow their issues to control their lives.

Allan was not immune to women with weird-ass issues. He went to the same seminary as I, and had been around his fair share of granola. So it was one of his highest compliments when he said to me, "Shannon, you know what I like about you? You don't have any weird-ass issues."

And I knew exactly what he meant.

Allan had some great ideas at times and when we discussed them, we'd hit a point of synergy where the ideas just flowed. When we started planning worship for preview services at Lighthouse (we worshiped together with our launch team about five months before our scheduled grand opening or launch), Allan wanted our altar tables decorated with the theme of the sermon series he was preaching. One week we were discussing the Holy Spirit so we wanted some dry ice to steam up from a bowl on the altar so that it would look like *the Spirit of God hovering over the waters*. Another time we were talking about being created *for such a time as this* and we had a huge clock in front of the altar.

When we began worship planning for the launch of Lighthouse, he wanted to use the idea that our church was a blank canvas. We had so many possibilities in front of us and we could make this church into anything we wanted. As I said before, we had blank canvases on each side of the altar where people came forward and put the initials or names of people that they knew who could benefit from a church focused on creative worship and mission in the world. Those canvases were then made into quilts that we put in our gathering area as a reminder that our church is not about *us* but about reaching other people.

It was brilliant, but it was his idea. When we had our launch service and Allan wasn't with us, it was hard to convey this idea to others. As I prepared for the sermon, all of my hidden weird-ass issues came to the surface. While I was thinking about telling people that we had a blank slate to start with, I felt as though our slate was stained with Allan's blood, haunting us as the *church where the pastor died*. And each time I thought about this, I became a blubbering idiot who was in no way capable of leading a congregation into a grace-filled life with Jesus that would be filled with hope.

I know that pastors say this often, but the wonder of that day was truly a God thing. I'm not sure what a *God thing* is, but a number of people that day spoke to God's glory. Many were there to support Allan's dream. Some were there seeking God. Others were there because they believed in the vision. Regardless of the reason, I know that I felt the Spirit of God that day and that is the only way I could have gotten through delivering the message.

I'd like to say that things went smoothly after that. I'd love to tell you that we had the great foundation of a happy and healthy church family, but I'm not sure I could stretch the truth that far. We did have about 125 the next week and had the start of some great new relationships among new families.

Then the granola showed up. Just as fruits, flakes, and nuts make up granola, church stalkers, enablers, and co-dependents, make up church granola. I've had people threaten me, accuse me of breaking up marriages, and tell me that we should be reaching out to the rich people in the community so that we can increase our budget.

These are the poster children for the *why I don't go to church* crowd. If you were to meet one of these people, why on earth would you want to be part of this same organization. On the other hand, if you meet the uber-Christians who believe they are on the road to perfection and are much closer to it than you are, they make you realize your inadequacies and wonder why you're part of the church as well.

I try to keep my weird-ass issues to things that don't involve relationship makers or breakers. My weird-ass church issues have to do with *things*. The first one that comes to mind is balloons. I have a minor phobia when it comes to latex balloons. Mylar ones are fine and I even enjoy latex helium ones as decorations. I think they are quite pretty. But if you were to put a latex balloon in the hands of a six year old boy, I might have a minor breakdown. The fear of popping and the noises that come with a child playing with a balloon make me as anxious as a chicken at Chick-fil-A. Most of the time this is not a problem; I can hide it for a while. But at some point the youth or children will do a game that involves balloons. For some reason we have large crowds of children those days and every one of them comes into the gathering area with a balloon in hand.

Another one of my issues is bathrooms. I have a rating system when it comes to public bathrooms. Waffle House is usually never above a three out of ten. The Ritz-Carlton in Buckhead, Georgia, is the highest standard at ten out of ten. When it comes to church bathrooms, I feel that our ability to make new disciples and transform the world is directly related to our bathroom décor and friendliness. Men usually don't understand this issue of mine and think that as long as it is clean, a bathroom should rate at least a nine. Bathrooms should be clean, well stocked with toilet paper, soap, and paper towels (although real, one time use towels or wash cloths get extra points).

Lotion, greenery, a hint of air freshener, and updated décor are all things that push a bathroom up the Karafanda scale and onto perfection.

Which brings me to my last weird-ass issue – poop. At some point, I gave a talk to a youth ministry group and talked about potty training my youngest son. At the time, the talk was going very poorly and everyone was tuning out. When I started discussing poop, everyone perked up and listened and I was able to keep their attention until the very end. Since then, poop has made an appearance in many of my sermons. It may be childish and crude, but sometimes you'll do whatever it takes to win people over to the love of God!

There you have it. The evolution of my weird-ass issues. From balloons popping and making me pee in my pants → to bathrooms rated on a Karafanda scale of awesomeness → to bathroom humor and how the word *poop* always seems to get attention.

Allan was wrong. I do have weird-ass issues. I just hide them fairly well. We all have weird-ass issues. All of us have things that make us unique in wonderful ways and things that make us unique in strange ways.

The great thing about weird-ass issues is that God loves us no matter what. God could not care less that you tell your pastor what she should wear on Sunday or that you yell at innocent children because they have a balloon in their hands. God loves you no matter what your weird-ass issues are. He sees you as the person you were created to be and in the moment that Allan told me I didn't have any weird-ass issues, I believe that Allan saw me as God does. If we could all do the same, we really would transform the world.

Above all, love each other deeply, because love covers a multitude of sins.
—*1 Peter 4:8, NIV*

Chapter 4: The Big Ask

<u>SYNERGISM</u> *broadly* **:** combined action or operation

You know that Seinfeld episode where they go to the party and everyone is assigned a different job during the party? It seems like a funny and odd thing to do, but did you notice how proud each person was about their job?

Allan's idea of hospitality was different from many others. He wanted to make sure that anyone and everyone who was at an event (church, youth, Vacation Bible School etc.), had a job. If you showed up only five minutes early and asked how you could help you may only be guarding the water fountain or pointing people to the restrooms, but you had a job. Having a job makes people feel important. It makes people feel like they've contributed to the success of a mission.

As soon as Allan died, I turned the office into a *war room*. I wanted EVERYONE to have a job for our grand opening I had huge pieces of sticky paper plastered all over the office. At the top I labeled areas that needed attention and then I numbered the amount of people I'd need for each task. I even had a few jobs saved in case I had someone come up to me at the last minute looking for something to do.

I've had arguments with other people who don't think that people who aren't in church are looking for a place to serve or even know that they have to serve. I agree that they may not express this need, but I feel that everyone wants to contribute to something. If they can't find that in the church, they'll look for it elsewhere such as at work or in their kids' activities.

Most people think hospitality means they are to serve others and *pamper* others so they feel loved and they'll want to come back. In a sense I see that we want to ensure that everyone is comfortable. But I feel that if someone comes to a church function then, on some level, they are seeking a place to belong. Giving them the opportunity to serve helps them feel a part of the family and lets them know they are needed.

I'm a BIG believer in free will. I mean, what's the point

otherwise. I have a brain that God gave me so I believe he wants me to use it to decide right from wrong and to choose to love Him.

But I had a professor in seminary who gave the only good argument I've ever heard against free will. He said that from the day we are born we are influenced by something. First our parents tell us what to do, how to act, how to dress. Then our friends, teachers, TV, radio, internet, and so many other things influence our thinking. So every time we make a decision we are influenced by these people or things. No one has totally free will because everything else in their life is driving his or her decisions.

If that's the case, then evangelism would be easy. It would just be a matter of marketing and brainwashing. There would be no need for personal relationships. No need for outreach events. If this were the case, it would relieve a lot of pressure from my job.

But I don't believe it's that easy. I think that people often surprise us by their actions and do things that just aren't the expectation of how they were brought up or how everyone else does things. We were made in God's image, and that includes having free will.

Because of free will, it is difficult to lead people to a relationship with Jesus. What seems so obvious to me – following a loving, powerful, creative God that wants me to be the person I was created to be – just doesn't seem logical to other people. And once they do decide that Christianity is for them, it is sometimes still difficult to get them to do something – anything in the church.

Allan on the other hand had a knack for getting people to do things. First of all, he wasn't a plan-ahead kind of guy. At least not the kind of plan-ahead person I am. I will plan every second and every resource out before the event. Allan would wait until the event started to assign jobs and he'd get everyone who showed up to do something. It was his way of connecting people. Making sure everyone had a job.

Of course for ongoing things, Allan would need people to plan, think ahead, and be in charge of a ministry. Usually he had someone in mind. He'd make sure he had a strong relationship with this person then would call him or her in for a special meeting or lunch, and lay out what he had in mind (such as teaching Sunday school or chaperoning a youth mission trip). He'd give the pros and the cons of what was going to happen (pro – your life will be changed by getting to know these kids; con – you'll feel older than you've ever felt). And then he'd say that he wanted that person to pray about it and think about it and that he'd be in touch. A week or so later he'd have another meeting and ask their response. He almost always got a yes.

Allan called this *The Big Ask*. At some point you need to just ask for what you want from someone. Don't expect them to know what needs to happen and don't expect them to want to do it at first.

I get the feeling that this is how I should be leading people to Jesus. Develop a relationship first. Then at some point, I just need to ask them if they are interested in being a Christian right now. We've got to get over our fear of the stigmatized, evangelical Christian and our fear of invitation. We may get shot down. But if we've developed that relationship ahead of time, not much has to change. We just let them know that the offer's always there. And we are there for them too, just as God is always there as well.

In many ways the weeks after Allan's death were a time that I questioned my call. But then I remembered back to the first time I had *The Big Ask* conversation with Allan and I remembered I was called to greatness. God had called me to join Him in doing amazing things in this world and that is always a call to greatness – not because of me, but because of Him. I began to realize that people see the Holy Spirit in me and they understand my potential. There were so many possibilities for me and I was ready to take at least one of them.

Don't burn out; keep yourselves fueled and aflame. Be alert servants of the Master, cheerfully expectant. Don't quit in hard times; pray all the harder. Help needy Christians; be inventive in hospitality.
—Romans 12:11, The Message

Chapter 5: Organizational Systems

Synergy is the creation of a whole that is greater than the sum of its parts.
—Ray French, Charlotte Rayner, Gary Rees, Sally Rumbles, et al., *Organizational Behaviour (2008)*

    Allan had a crazy organizational system. He would take a yellow legal pad to every meeting he had in order to take notes. When he was done, he usually would file the entire pad away in a file folder. Unfortunately he didn't always have the same idea as to where to put things. Sometimes office equipment would go under "O"; other times it would be under "P" for phones or "A" for AT&T. When we cleaned up the office after his death, we discovered that there were about 20 or so legal pads that had only one or two pages written on that had been filed away. We took those pages off and put the legal pad away with the others in the office supply closet. When all was said and done, we passed out 60 different empty legal pads to innocent people who knew not from whence they came.

    Everyone has their own style. I prefer most of my organizing to be done on my smart phone but I still need a bit of the tactile feeling that comes with writing things down on paper. Some are highly organized with a paper only system.

    The key to being organized as a team is to learn the style of each person on the team. Some people do well with verbal instructions and no follow up. Others need the email reminder. Holding their hand is a bit too close to micromanaging but you get the drift.

    Organization is a Biblical concept. God created the important stuff in seven days. On day one, two and three he created the space for the stuff he created on days four, five and six. There is a time and a season for everything.

    After Allan's death the organizational Nazi in me came out. My organizational skills were the only thing getting me through starting a new church while mourning a great friend. I put everything I had into my job for the next few weeks for two very important reasons: 1) I was determined to keep the vision going and to make sure that our dream stayed alive. Allan may have not been alive but by golly I was going to keep moving forward no matter what God gave me. And 2) organizing my days this way was honestly the only thing giving me purpose and hope. At a time when I couldn't feel who I was anymore, I felt that my daily ministry tasks were keeping my identity real. I was still vital to something if not someone. Each day I had something to do whether it was cleaning out Allan's office to make room for a new pastor or emailing reminders to our setup team for the week. I filled up my day with checklists and all the while I knew what those checklists were doing. They were delaying a meltdown that I needed and craved but was not ready to have. I wanted to be strong for my congregation and my family until I knew it was safe to let go. The office was my safe place and, without Allan, my safe place had turned to Jell-O and all it was going to take was one meltdown for my illusion of safety to melt away.

I've never felt more emotionally and spiritually fragile in my life than during this time period. As much as I'd like to argue against it, you cannot organize yourself into emotional health and spiritual maturity. You can organize the tools that will help, but the organization will only get you so far. There weren't enough yellow pads in the world to bring Big Al back into my life so I began the task of mentally organizing a life without him, because I just wasn't ready to live a life without him.

When Joab saw he was under attack in front and behind, he took the select troops of Israel and organized them for combat against the Arameans.
—2 Samuel 10:9, GOD'S WORD

Chapter 6: Unbalanced

A designed beauty of synergy is that it serves only to add, never subtract.
—*Barb Rententbach, Synergy (2009)*

Before we started Lighthouse together, Allan and I had worked in youth ministry at another church. He was staff. I was a volunteer. He took me out to Waffle House for one of his famous *Big Ask* moments. I'm not sure what he was asking, but I know I said yes. It was hard to say no to him.

As we ordered that day, he asked for three eggs – two of them scrambled and one of them raw, still in the shell and delivered at the end of the meal. When I gave him the *whatyoutalkinbout* eye, he explained that he was hosting a thank you dinner for the staff at our church and still needed to make a cheesecake. He had discovered that morning that he only had four eggs and needed five. So instead of cutting our meeting short to go to the grocery store, he devoted his full attention to me and ordered a raw egg to-go at Waffle House.

Allan was always throwing celebration parties, welcoming dinners, or just impromptu restaurant gatherings. Walking into one of these events was like the previously mentioned episode of Seinfeld where Elaine tried to get rid of Putty's fur coat. The host of that party gave everyone a job and Elaine was in charge of coats. Other people at the party also had jobs such as making sure guests didn't tap on the fish tank, filling the ice bucket, preventing certain people from talking to each other, etc.

Allan did the exact same thing at his gatherings. When people walked in, most of them asked if they could help. Most of the time it is just easier to have everything ready before the party starts, but Allan always had one or two chores he could assign such as getting the party trash can out of the garage and lining it with the special liners. If someone was lingering on the fringes of the room and looking as if they weren't mingling well, he'd ask them to help out with a multi-person task so they would strike up a conversation while they got to work.

To Allan, hospitality was providing each person a place to

serve to give them a sense of ownership and make them feel they were part of the team. My idea of hospitality is to do jobs for them. Feeling overwhelmed by taking care of all your kids? I'll plan a Girls Night Out for us! Want to become a better student? I'll organize your agenda and schedule all of your upcoming tasks. Need some spiritual training? I'll put you on a plan of Bible reading and prayer that will knock the socks off the Holy Spirit.

Allan and I were different. We complimented each other. We were a team. He would give people jobs and I would organize them. Our love for other people in the name of God pushed us to show hospitality in our own radical ways. We wanted people to feel the right amount of comfort and the right amount of belonging.

After his death, I wanted so much to keep this core value of hospitality going at Lighthouse, but it felt so lopsided. I had a hard time welcoming others when I wasn't feeling welcome myself. I had other people supporting me, but I didn't have balance. I felt like I didn't have a job (or at least not the same one I signed on for), so I waited for God to, once again, show me how to be the person He called me to be. I waited and continued to do both jobs for #1 (the Senior Pastor) and #2 (the Associate Pastor).

Instead, he must be hospitable, love what is good, use good judgment, be fair and moral, and have self-control.
—Titus 1:8, GOD'S WORD

Chapter 7: Drugs and Disney

***syn·er·gy** [sin-er-jee]* noun, plural *syn·er·gies*.
Biochemistry, Pharmacology . The cooperative action of two
or more stimuli or drugs.

     Pastors love to preach about the call of God. Mostly because our call sounds so vague and we are scared that no one will understand or accept what we've heard. The first time I felt called, I was in the church van going to a Sunday School training event. The Associate Pastor was driving and started talking about her call to ministry. I was only half paying attention when I felt a sudden rush of emotion. I got chills all over and started quietly sobbing. I felt like my world was changing but no one around me noticed. I couldn't for the life of me understand how no one else in the van was not affected. I wanted to desperately talk to someone about it, but couldn't quite get the words out.
     Several times during that year I had the same nagging feeling that God was calling me to ministry. When I did finally decide to talk about it, I went to see the Associate Pastor that had told her story in the van. After I told her all the things that I'd noticed over the past year she didn't look at me funny. She didn't think I was crazy. She just sighed a happy sigh and told me that God was calling me; I needed to go to seminary and I needed to be ordained. Then she asked me a series of questions that validated that she really wasn't crazy either. Was I losing sleep over this? Did it sometimes make me sick? Did I try to volunteer more to make the feeling go away? Did it ring through my head at all hours?
     I answered yes to all. She knew what I was going through and had talked to many others going through the same thing.

I can also remember the exact moment God called me to Lighthouse. I was sitting at someone's kitchen table and heard another person say that new churches are the quickest way to reach new believers and suddenly I heard this voice saying, "Call Allan Todd. Call Allan Todd. Call Allan Todd. Go to the Lighthouse. Go to the Lighthouse!"

And at that moment I knew that it was from God.

The origin of other calls is harder to discern. After Allan died I conveniently postponed my breakdown for six weeks after his funeral. The Cabinet of the United Methodist Church would be meeting then to decide our new pastor and I needed to keep it all together until after that decision was made and before he or she got there. I was doing really well with that plan. I had many moments where I was sad and I was working with someone to get through the stress but, so far, no meltdown.

The day that our Cabinet was supposed to appoint our new pastor to Lighthouse I received a call that I was anticipating and dreading at the same time. My District Superintendent (or DS) called to say that they hadn't appointed anyone to Lighthouse. She wanted me to think about my call to ministry and see if God was calling me to take on this position. I was ecstatic. I had been waiting for her to call me and tell me who our new pastor was and I was dreading the idea that it might be someone that I couldn't work with or that didn't think in innovative ways. I could work with me. I understood Lighthouse. I had more invested than anyone else. Of course I could do this.

But on the other hand, how could I be the one to replace Allan? Who had been closer to him and how could I separate myself from the role of Associate Pastor?

I had a lot to think about. This not only would affect Lighthouse, but also my family and my call to ministry.

Unfortunately, I didn't get details on what to tell the congregation. They were all waiting for the news because they knew a decision would be made. The next day I did something incredibly stupid. I was completely honest. I told them what was going on and that I needed their prayers as well as prayers for the Cabinet as they still pondered this decision.

The next day, just when I was starting to feel good about

things, I got another call. One that I'd just as soon forget.

My DS told me that she'd received an email from someone in my church saying that they didn't think I'd be a good fit. They thought I was not outgoing enough or friendly enough. I should have only communicated to my congregation that the Cabinet was still looking at options. I had upset my DS and I had to deal with the fact that someone from my church family really didn't like me. I'm not here for everyone to like me. But I'd just taken this church through one of the worst things that a church can go through. I'd literally put my sweat and tears into it and my soul ached with the disappointment I was feeling. It was at this moment that my scheduled breakdown got moved up to the immediate present and hit me with full force.

I hung up the phone and wailed. Not just cried, but screamed out loud and I finally asked the question I never thought I'd ask – *Why*? Before this moment it didn't matter why. Knowing wouldn't help and I probably couldn't understand anyway. But for some reason screaming *Why?* at the top of my voice was the only thing my confused heart could do to release pressure and angst that had been welling up in me. I hurt. Not only for my loss, but for some sort of betrayal that I was feeling, and for disappointment in myself for not being able to handle this one last straw.

To this day I both bless and curse the person that sent that email. I hate what I had to go through. I hate the fact that I had to make such a horrible decision between furthering my church and replacing my best friend. But I praise the fact that my meltdown, which I had so carefully put off, came at exactly the right time.

After I calmed down a bit, I called my DS. She was very supportive as I said that I was honored and felt that I could absolutely do a wonderful job in this position, however, there was no way that I could do it now because of my emotional state. I would be doing it for ALL the wrong reasons. I told her that we needed someone as soon as possible. Then I hung up the phone, finished my meltdown, and finally started to mourn.

Again, I felt that hole in my heart. I kept thinking each night that I would wake up and it would be filled. I asked God to fill it, but He just surrounded it. It hurt so much. The thought of waking up again dancing was a distant memory and I asked God to please let me know it would be alright.

Before our new pastor came to Lighthouse, our family went on vacation to Disney World. As we walked through the park, I knew something was horribly wrong. The happiest place on earth was just a distraction for me. My mind stayed occupied just enough to forget the pain, but every time we left the park and I got back to the condo, I slept or I cried. In a dark room, while my family was having fun at the swimming pool, I lay on the bed and stared into nothingness for hours, and I didn't care if I ever snapped out of it.

When I got back home, I realized I was feeling quite sick. I was having sharp stomach pains that could not be traced to diet or a change in routine. My doctor ran some tests and nothing appeared to be wrong. I had been going to a counselor since Allan's death because I knew it would help and because a friend of mine told me she would nag me until I went. It really wasn't healthy for me to lead a congregation onto perfection without getting some help during this time. After a few sessions and my not so happy Disney trip, I talked to the counselor and later the doctor about anti-depressants.

I didn't want a crutch. I didn't want a quick fix. I just wanted things to be normal again and I didn't want to have to take a pill to do it. But I couldn't deny that my mourning had become more serious and was beginning to affect my physical health as well. When I finally told my doctor that in addition to my symptoms, I had suffered this terrible loss and that I thought I might be depressed, he immediately prescribed an anti-depressant and was 90% certain that my pains would ease away once I started taking them.

He was right. After two weeks my stomach pains were gone. I no longer sat on my sofa for periods of time that escaped me and kept me from living the life God gave me. I still hurt. I still mourned. But I could cope and it made all the difference.

I was able to once again try and live out my calling. My calling certainly looked different than I ever imagined it would be. But now when someone confesses to me that they are on medication for depression, I understand. When someone comes to me and tells me they've lost someone close, I understand. When someone comes to me and tells me they feel that a friend has turned on them, I understand.

I understand because I've been there. I never want to go back, but it makes me who I am and helps me to know that I am a human in need of God's grace.

We have different gifts, according to the grace given to each of us. If your gift is prophesying, then prophesy in accordance with your faith.
—*Romans 12:6, NIV*

Chapter 8: Saying Good-Bye

Synergy—the bonus that is achieved when things work together harmoniously.
—*Mark Twain*

Every New Year's Eve I have a big dilemma: to sleep or not to sleep. I'm one of those people that *needs* at least 8 hours of sleep and thinks that 10:00 pm is staying up late. So every New Year's Eve, I wonder if I'll make it until midnight. When I was oh so younger (a teenager or in my early 20s) I felt as if this made me really boring, but as I got older, had babies, and valued sleep even more, I decided that it's just another day, just another year, and why not get off on the right foot with a good night's sleep.

I also stopped resolutions. If a resolution is not worth starting right now (as opposed to waiting for the New Year), then it's probably not worth doing. But one tradition that I have kept up is my own personal year in review. At first this was just a mental exercise but then it turned into a scrapbooking project and, finally, to a home movie montage.

When I started completing my 2006 scrapbook, I kept thinking – what a crappy year. I'd gone through loss like never before and my emotions hadn't completely healed yet. But as I started putting all the events together from the year I realized that to call the year crappy was an insult to Allan and many other people. It was actually a great year. Our church launched; my baby started Kindergarten; I met many new friends, and had some wonderful adventures.

Never let one bad thing color your life. It can shape and mold you, but it shouldn't keep you in the state of emotions that it inflicts.

It is strange to think about final words. You know the question, "If you had one day left to live, what would you do differently? What would you say to the people you love?"

It is a bit ironic that I mentioned this in a sermon just a few months before Allan's death. The next day he told me that it was the topic of conversation at his house. He told me he wouldn't really do anything differently as long as it was with his family.

The day before Allan died he spent some time with me. I feel blessed in a way but I'll also never forget one thing he told me. Of all the parting words of wisdom, this is the one I remember...

I let it be known that I'm not a huge fan of country music. Don't get me wrong, there are several country artists and songs that I keep on my iPod but, as a whole, it wouldn't be my first choice of music stations. Upon hearing this, Allan turned (while driving), looked me straight in the eye and said, "You're going to hell."

I replied, "If there's only country music playing in heaven, then it's not my idea of heaven."

He said, "Doesn't matter anyway. I'll be up there listening to God's music while you'll be in hell."

Amazing that his parting words of wisdom still make me laugh.

The first summer after Lighthouse's launch, we put on a Vacation Bible School for the kids. The theme was *Avalanche Ranch*, a country theme that we did in a church member's barn. All of the songs had a country sound to them. I laughed at the irony and felt that Allan was up there laughing at me as I enjoyed seeing all the kids grow closer to God. I've been much more tolerant of country music since.

The week of the first anniversary of Allan's death, I had to say *good-bye* several times. First there was a family reunion. It was great to get together, but in the end, we all said good-bye and I knew that I wouldn't see some of them again until next year.

I also had to say good-bye to the covenant group of pastors that I had been meeting with during the year. Although I see all these people once a year or more, I would never get to spend time with them in this setting again and, in a small way, this made me really sad. We had grown close like family, and shared great, deep feelings. I was blessed to have had them there during that time of my life.

Finally I said good-bye with someone in our church who lost her father. I never knew him, but said good-bye all the same. I hurt for her and her brothers and the pain they felt from celebrating their dad's life and, also, remembering their mother who had died a time long ago. In a strange way, it is always a blessing to be there for someone when they mourn a death.

I don't know how people without faith say good-bye. For me, saying good-bye is a celebration of who we are, a reflection of the transition we're going through at the time, and a blessing for the future. It does make us remember our good times and helps us seal those memories in our hearts. Good-byes are hard because we want to say so much and yet there are not always words to express our feelings.

So I need to stop and say *I love you.* I write this for those I have loved, loved and lost, and so that others can find love—hopefully through God, and also through others expressing God's love. So again I say, *I love you.* and may all your good-byes be blessings.

On August 3, 2007 at 9:18 a.m., I had officially not seen Allan Todd for over one year. Last time I saw him, he was in a white painting outfit – covered in various blotches of paint. No doubt an outfit he had had for years; an outfit marked by time and events. Mission trips, rental properties he owned, different rooms of his house, probably an outfit that could tell a good story. Lesson learned – always watch what you wear as it could stick in someone's memory as the last hideous thing that someone saw you in.

It was such an amazing year in so many ways. I preached the weekend before Lighthouse's one year anniversary. We were doing a series on heroes and I preached on Esther. I don't think anyone ever put together that we had a *Such A Time As This* series the year before and had a similarly angled series about people in the Bible at the right place at the right time. I didn't even pick up on it until halfway through. I talked about Esther as a fairy tale. When you read the story, it actually is quite Disney. Her parents are gone. She's a commoner. She's beautiful. And she ends up saving the day. I tried to get a good definition of what a hero is and how Esther was one. Brave? Noble? Takes action? Nothing seemed appropriate for a hero. Then I finally came up with an angle I liked. Stupid! There's such a fine line between doing something stupid and doing something heroic. It was kind of stupid for Esther to go to the King when it was against the law for her to go without an invitation AND knowing that the last Queen was killed for disobedience. But she did it anyway and that made her a hero.

I think some people would say that starting a church without the Senior Pastor is stupid. In fact I think it's ridiculous to think that this would work. But we did it. I don't know if that made us heroes.

We certainly kept the vision. We definitely have changed lives for the better. We had moments where we experienced God and we saw a glimpse of what the world could be like if we let love rule our hearts above anything else.

And who of us are the heroes? Me? I'll take it if I deserve it. Our new Senior Pastor? He must have had patience, love, compassion, and an intensity for God in order to lead us through this. The people of Lighthouse? Definitely. Okay, so some of them I could throw out the window at times. But then there's that core group of people. Those people that I believed saved my sanity during the first year after Allan's death. The people that were there for me when I cried. Made me laugh when I needed to. Carried me when I just couldn't get up. And, better yet, did the same for total strangers all year long because of their love for God. I hope they know who they are. I hope I've told them or expressed some gratitude.

I'm not sure we can ever express to someone (while they're alive or dead) the gratitude we have for them. Allan helped make me the person I am today. In fact, he brought out so many of the good parts in me that were just waiting to escape.

I'm not sure I wanted to be created *for such a time as this*. I think I'd have given anything to have had the experience of one more year with him. God didn't give me a say. But He was there helping me out along the way.

I can't believe it took me a whole year just to say good-bye. I told someone about the hole in my heart, a void where he once was that just ached. She told me that as painful as that is, I probably didn't ever want that hole to close. She's right. It's not quite as painful but the void is still there and it reminds me of who he was and what we started. I will never, ever, never forget the dreams, the vision, the fun. Because they were all part of a Divine intersection. A time when God came down to us and showed us what He wanted. How lucky were we? That kind of thing doesn't happen every day and we were so blessed to be a part of it. I see now that God is going to keep blessing Lighthouse because it really is part of His plan. I may question those plans sometimes (okay daily), but I can't believe that I'm actually doing something that pleases God. I know that we all try to do that every day, but this was big scale. This was world changing!

I will never doubt again that a small group of people can change the world. Because, indeed, we've done it.

I write this to you whose experience with God is as life-changing as ours, all due to our God's straight dealing and the intervention of our God and Savior, Jesus Christ. Grace and peace to you many times over as you deepen in your experience with God and Jesus, our Master.
—*2 Peter 1:2, The Message*

Part Two: New Life Lessons
***
Chapter 9: First Impressions

The greatest benefit of synergy is born in the diversity of perspectives. The highest value can be found in these variances. Too much of the same does not create change in the same way, does not produce the sweetest fruits for all, and gets old quick.
—*Danielle Marie Crume*

    In October of 2006 I went to a large conference for church leadership. There were 10,000 people in the arena worshipping God and celebrating what God was doing, and all I could focus on was one thing – who was coming to Lighthouse to be the senior pastor. I sat with another clergy friend who would find out the information just as soon as I would. Even though I was learning some awesome things about leadership and being reminded that God has my back, my mind was still on the meeting that would decide the future of Lighthouse.

    I prayed. I prayed like never before. *God please be in that room and part of that process. God, please don't let them put someone stupid here. God, please let the person appointed here understand the things that are going on around me at this conference. God, please let the person appointed have a great heart. God, please hurry up and help the Cabinet make the decision.*

    I remember seeing the caller ID when my DS called to tell me the news. Mark Jordan was joining us. I felt relieved. I didn't know who Mark was so I knew he couldn't be a total dork or he would have stood out. But at least I had a name. I now knew.

    And yet I knew nothing. So I did what anyone else would do. I cyber stalked him. When the conference was over our Youth Director, Kevin, and I got to a laptop as fast as we could and looked up Mark Jordan and his former churches. What we saw was good. He was young, part of a new contemporary church, and had a passion for theater. I was a thespian in high school and Kevin had acquired the bug in his twenties so we knew we had something in common with him.

A few weeks later I was to meet Mark for the first time. I wanted to make a good impression. I wanted him to be able to trust me and listen to me so that we could work well together. The only thing holding me back was that I was still in a fragile state.

I decided to call him before he met with everyone else. I wanted to see if there was anything I could do for him before he came down later that night.

We exchanged a nice conversation. He seemed so caring. And maybe I was reading into things, but I thought he might actually *think outside the box*. We talked about contemporary worship and new churches and our families for a bit. I told him that I went to Candler, but that I didn't have any weird-ass issues (not sure I used those words, but I alluded to it).

Later that night, I met him for the first time in a group with about ten other people. Everyone seemed to like him. It was great. I should have been relieved… but then I noticed I wasn't. I was feeling something kind of strange. I was jealous. Not jealous that he was our new pastor and people liked him, but I was upset that we were all at the same starting line—kind of a reverse jealousy. I was jealous for what I didn't have. Everyone else at Lighthouse knew just as much about Mark as I did and that bothered me. I wanted to know him better than everyone. I wanted to be able to answer for him when people asked a question. I wanted to know what he would say before he would say it.

I wanted my relationship with Mark to pick up where my relationship with Allan left off. I wanted someone to ask me a question and I would have no doubt how Mark would feel about it. I wanted a synergy that could create ideas when the two of us discussed ministry. I wanted a new office spouse. I felt the painful reminder that I was starting over and I just didn't feel up to the task.

Luckily I had a few more weeks. My family and I took some time off and I was ready when Mark started. I enjoyed helping him unpack his office. He seemed to have just as many toys to play with as he did theology books to read.

You can tell a lot about someone by looking at their office. Offices seem to fall into three basic categories.

First, there are the *sparse and clean* offices. These are the IKEA offices. The ones that you see in catalogues where the pens are all the same size, color, and brand, perfectly arranged in a beautiful pewter holder. This is the office where OCD people live. There is no personality but it does get the job done. Everything is at right angles and nothing is brought into the office that doesn't go with the preset color scheme.

Secondly, you have the *sloppy but categorized* office. These offices are the Albert Einstein offices. In this office you would see books everywhere and papers everywhere but the owner of the office would be able to find anything within a few seconds. Books may not be turned the same way but would be categorized on the shelf (or floor) according to the office inhabitant's mind. These are the type of offices that make me cringe. I have no idea how they get any work done but, at the same time, they fascinate me. To be able to work in chaos like this is almost God-like.

Finally, you have the *mysterious and fun* office. This creative setting is my kind of office. Most of these offices contain at least one of the following: a Pez dispenser, a fart machine, a Staples *Easy* button, some action figure, a Rubik's cube, or a favorite childhood toy. Each thing in this office has a story. It gives a launching point for greater conversation and keeps kids of all ages entertained in what would otherwise be a stuffy setting.

My office currently has a plethora of sock monkeys, a Jesus-feeds-the-five-thousand action figure, a Pastor Barbie, a drawer full of candy, a fart machine desperately in need of batteries, and a Jesus doll that resembles a Cabbage Patch doll and kind of freaks people out (but that children seem to love).

When Mark unpacked, he had a Darth Vader button that he pushed to show he was in a bad mood, a Superman clock, a Spiderman action figure, and various Disney characters hidden about but were easy to find to the expert *Where's Waldo* fan.

I knew at that moment it would be easy to get to know Mark. You don't have that kind of office if you want to keep things a secret. People who are hard to get to know (at least for me) have the Ikea office or the Einstein office. Every time I went into his office, I would see a new toy and ask him about it. His answer always gave me a clue about who he was.

But there was still one question that needed to be asked and I was terrified of the answer.

Allan had been a huge Florida Gator fan. There were several trinkets in his office showing his pride in his team. His father had been on staff at the University of Florida so he literally grew up near and on campus.

My office had several tributes to my team as well. I had a few Georgia Tech trinkets and, of course, my diploma, of which I was very proud.

As I looked around Mark's office, I didn't see any leanings one way or the other. Most Georgia natives either bleed red and black for the University of Georgia or white and gold for Georgia Tech. Mark had gone to Georgia State before they had a football team.

I guess I was scared of the answer. If he pulled for UGA, this would be one strike that I couldn't resolve. He had the right office. He had the right attitude. But what if he didn't have the right team?

All I could do was ask. After a few weeks, I finally asked what team he pulled for. I'll never forget his reaction. He was so scared of hurting my feelings that he kind of looked down and shuffled his feet. He seemed to be taking the route a politician does when confronted on a hot button topic that they've flip-flopped on. Finally he just said, "Well my team isn't doing so well this year."

This was one of those happy years for Tech fans when UGA did poorly and Tech was winning. For some reason, after finding out that he was a UGA fan, I didn't like him any less. In fact, it gave our congregation great balance and I also saw how Mark's compassion in knowing how important it is to find common ground was going to lead us to some great healing.

I was no longer jealous. What's more, I took that first step I had been holding back until that moment. I opened myself up to expose our differences. Until that point, I focused on our similarities. I believed that if we were alike, it would be easier to move on. I was forgetting was it is impossible to move on with God's work if people are all the same. We were building the body of Christ, not from scratch, but a new congregation among the body. We needed as many different and diverse people as possible to reach the different and diverse people in our community. When I finally got to a point of celebrating our differences and letting myself be vulnerable to getting to know someone, I felt as though I was finally able to lead Lighthouse forward because that is exactly how you make disciples.

The priest is to take from her hands the grain offering for jealousy, wave it before the LORD and bring it to the altar.
—Numbers 5:25, NIV

Chapter 10: Answering Your Own Questions

Ineffective people live day after day with unused potential. They experience synergy only in small, peripheral ways in their lives. But creative experiences can be produced regularly, consistently, almost daily in people's lives. It requires enormous personal security and openness and a spirit of adventure.
—*Stephen R. Covey*

    Mark is an excellent preacher. I think the first Sunday he was at Lighthouse we all held our breath. We'd met him and knew he was nice and sympathetic. We understood that he knew how to handle and even preferred a contemporary church. But we had no idea what we were in store for regarding Sunday messages.

    Church was full that day. A lot of people were there for curiosity, support, and healing. We went through the songs and got to the moment of the sermon. I don't know at what point it happened, and I'm not positive it happened for everyone but, for me, there was definitely a sigh of relief. Mark could effectively communicate the Gospel.

    Wait. No, that makes him sound just adequate. Mark was engaging, funny, sympathetic, understanding and memorable. Sometimes when I preach, I often wonder what impact it will have. Will anyone remember my words five minutes after they leave? To this day, I still remember Mark's first sermon at Lighthouse. He told the story of his vacation the week after he heard of Allan's death. He was at his mom's family vacation home in Canada and felt an uneasiness in his soul about his ministry. At that point he heard the small still voice of God say, "Go to the Lighthouse. Go to the Lighthouse."

    Mark, being the obedient servant, packed up his wife and son and drove to the nearby lighthouse. While he was there he prayed and listened. He didn't hear anything else but he knew all would be okay. When he got back home from vacation, he got a message telling him he was moving to The Lighthouse United Methodist Church.

    Mark made us feel okay that day. We were nowhere near ready

to feel joyful as we were still mourning. But we knew in that moment, God was still with us and we were fine. In fact, we were more than fine. We were doing what God called us all to do.

Mark's other sermons stand out as well. Mark has a performing arts background and occasionally will break into song during one of his sermons. He also likes to mention TV shows, movies, commercials, and other pop culture references, if they get the point across.

One Sunday he preached about possibilities. And then he broke into song singing the Campbell's soup commercial: *Campbell's mmm good. Possibilities.*

His message that day was about grace. With the grace of God we have so many possibilities. Mark is proof of God's grace. I honestly believe that if anyone else had been appointed at Lighthouse after Allan's death, we wouldn't have the possibilities we have now.

Not only could Mark prepare a good sermon but he was so in tune with the Holy Spirit that he could incorporate things around him very quickly. One Sunday, some child had left a Magna Doodle on stage. As he was preaching he reached down and picked it up and wrote *sin* on it and then erased it. I know that Jesus *erases* our sin but using the Magna Doodle that day made me think about it all week.

Not all preachers can preach. The number one fear that Americans have is the fear of speaking in public. If that statistic is correct, we probably have a bunch of pastors in America that live in fear of Sunday morning. I do believe that God can work through even the worst preacher. I know that there have been several mediocre sermons I have given that other people have told me helped them see something more clearly or think about something differently.

One of the things Mark does in some sermons is ask non-rhetorical questions. Many preachers ask deep, theological, rhetorical questions such as, "Why do bad things happen to good people?"

Mark asks easy, sometimes-theological questions that actually have answers. Usually when a preacher asks this question, they don't expect congregational participation. Mark would ask a question and then whisper the answer out of the corner of his mouth as if it had come from the congregation. Often someone would take the hint and repeat the answer and Mark would congratulate him or her for knowing the answer.

By answering his own questions, we were able to discern some real answers for ourselves. His sermons helped all of us grow in our faith and be the church that God called us to be. I don't think we ever realized how lucky we were that first Sunday. We needed desperately to hear Good News and because of Mark's gift, we heard it often.

Sometimes we need to ask the questions that we already know the answers to. Answering our own questions helps us to solidify our beliefs and express our faith. I'm not sure if Mark means more than just trying to energize the congregation. But when you use this technique as a personal practice, you show the world your certainty and clarify your position so that everyone can hear.

So faith comes from hearing, that is, hearing the Good News about Christ.
—Romans 10:17, NLT

Chapter 11: The Holy Spirit—A Hostage Situation

Successfully adding the popular characters from the 'Pirates of the Caribbean' films with the mythology of our classic attraction is an example of Disney synergy and Walt Disney Imagineering at its finest.
—*Jay Rasulo*

Allan always told me his number one rule when working for him – No Surprises! There's nothing worse than getting a call from someone in the congregation asking you about a situation that you are not aware of.

Of course, it is funny the things that people think you know. They often think I am a mind reader. I guess they think that since I'm a minister I must be closer to God and, therefore, God is sharing His omnipotence with me on all congregational situations. People assume that I know how much they've been giving, when they miss a tithe, how their marriage is going, what their kids' grades are in school, if they didn't like a sermon, what they are allergic to – literally, they'll assume you know anything!

Then there are the people that assume you are clueless and try to get away with stuff. They'll talk about you like the dog you are in the middle of a Bible study or they'll sigh and roll their eyes in the middle of the sermon or they'll send emails back and forth to someone and expect that you'll never find out. Gossip always gets around. Personal details about your life do not. If I broke my arm when I was seven, no one would know. If I broke my arm roller blading naked during a fraternity party last week, EVERYONE would know.

It may seem stupid or demeaning to give a report to the Lead Pastor or Church Board about every little detail you're doing, but keeping the pastor and church council informed goes a long way toward helping people see how I am contributing to the vision. It also helps the leaders of the church re-direct any questions my way instead of stepping too far into a mess I don't need to get involved with.

I was at a church once where I planned for our youth to visit some of the homebound in our congregation. It was a suggestion from one of the teenagers and I thought it would be a great way for them to get to know each other. After announcing that the youth wanted to do this, I had an involved mom email me and ask if I wanted her to get her husband to drive the church bus and for her to call a few different homebound people to visit. I was beginning to think I had hit the jackpot. I had a person volunteer for something without being asked first. As we got closer to the date, I asked our church secretary to put it in the bulletin. I put it in our youth newsletter, and it was on the website. I tend to over communicate if possible so that no one gets left behind. Apparently, I communicated more than was expected. The volunteering mom called me and jokingly reprimanded me. The date for our outing was three days after my birthday. She never intended to visit someone and was going to throw me a surprise party with the youth. She was smart enough to only tell one other adult and did not tell any youth who would blab at the first opportunity. I had no idea. And by promoting the event in all possible avenues, I unknowingly wrecked my own birthday party. Not all situations have such an interesting ending.

A few months after Lighthouse's launch, conflict reared its ugly head with a lovely church crisis. It really wasn't so much a crisis as an over dramatized situation. There was a particular person in the church who believed that the leadership of the church was driving the Holy Spirit out of all things.

It excited me that, perhaps, I could have such power. While I pondered how to use this new power, I became a bit disappointed. I was counting on the Holy Spirit to be there for me on Sundays, to talk to me through prayer and, frankly, help me with church drama. But since the Holy Spirit had been taken hostage by one of us, I guess I could no longer rely on the Holy Spirit for such things.

I can easily see how someone could give up the church (and knowingly or unknowingly God) just to get rid of the drama. Church is not supposed to be difficult in this way. It isn't supposed to be a burden. It is supposed to be an extension of Christ's work and a place to renew your spirit, not a place to validate agendas and criticize lifestyles. Fortunately this drama was short lived.

Or so we thought.

After crisis number one was smoothed over and relationships were restored, crisis number two came to surface. I would go into detail about all of these but honestly it was so overly dramatic then, why make it that way again? Plus, everything blends together in my head after a while so I'm not sure I could.

After a bit, the situation resolved itself and we realized that the Holy Spirit had been released to do its job. What most people don't realize is that by encouraging conflict or avoiding a healthy discussion of differences, they are the ones thwarting the movement of the Holy Spirit. When people aren't able to use the guidance of the Holy Spirit to help them settle accusations, they end up dividing the church and stalling the mission.

The Bible is clear about how to handle conflict and, by doing so, shows us that conflict is unavoidable. Disagreements will happen and even though no one desires these situations, there are ways to handle arguments. Matthew 18:15-17 is like the Church Human Resources Manual for church conflict. Its suggestions help us to get past our immediate problems but what we are left with (whether or not these actions are followed), are hurt feelings.

Even now, years later, I have to admit I can still feel the hurt from various situations in different churches. Conversely, I can feel the hurt left by others at churches before I even get there. Conflict is not the way to fulfill the mission of the church and until we are able to let the Holy Spirit heal us from these conflicts, we cannot move forward with the mission that God gave us in the first place.

We tend to remember that Jesus gave us the peace that passes all understanding, but forget that Jesus turned over the tables outside the Temple in anger. The idea is to fight for things that matter. The mission matters. Drama doesn't. And if you feel that someone is driving the Holy Spirit out of the room, look up. God is still there. The Holy Spirit can't be driven out that easily.

If a believer does something wrong, go confront him when the two of you are alone. If he listens to you, you have won back that believer. But if he does not listen, take one or two others with you so that every accusation may be verified by two or three witnesses. If he ignores these witnesses, tell it to the community of believers. If he also ignores the community, deal with him as you would a heathen or a tax collector.
—Matthew 18:15-17, GOD'S WORD

Chapter 12: Game On!

A lot of what we will do is get our arms around what we have. Look for ways to create synergy and then get everybody driving down the road in the same direction.
—*Don Snyder*

I was never an athletic person growing up. I loved to dance and took ballet for several years but other than that, I didn't do much physically. I also was never much of a sports fan until college and even then it took me years and a boyfriend who was an enthusiastic sports fan to get me to understand the difference between *shooting one and one* after being fouled or *shooting twice*. I still have no idea what *no pepper* means (even though it has been explained to me). And I still don't understand when a kick is on or offsides. It's all so confusing.

So when I took up running a few years after college, I surprised everyone, even myself. I needed to get in shape and went out one day and started running. I kept doing it almost every day and kept going farther and farther. Soon I was running 5K races. I finally understood the metric system and understood runner *speak*. I knew what a PR was and kept trying to get one. I got some great shoes and even splurged on running clothes. I wasn't a running fanatic and never really experienced a runner's high, but I really did enjoy it. I trained hard and enjoyed the races I entered.

Then one day it happened. The time I put into training paid off. I ran a 10K that was known for being flat. It was actually kind of easy. I felt like I had done well. When races are over there are snacks and freebies to choose from while you wait for the others to finish and winners to be announced. I usually grab my bagel or banana and head out. But for some reason, this time I lingered a bit longer and, sure enough, my moment came. I had placed 3rd in my age group! After that, every time I ran, I ran to win. It didn't happen often, but I knew it was possible and that knowledge made all of the training and hard work worth it.

The *getting to know you* stage of Mark's relationship with Lighthouse was bittersweet. On one hand we were a close congregation with a mind for mission but, on the other hand, we had some issues. There were particular individuals on both a congregational and conference level that questioned Mark's every move. And what was even harder was that sometimes these very same people would sing his praises one day, and then ask what he'd accomplished and where his faith was the next.

After a few months of this, Mark had had enough. He sat down and put on paper something that became known in closed quarters as The Lighthouse Manifesto. He wrote about all the good things that Lighthouse had, and articulated in more detail how we were going to accomplish the mission of the church. But instead of passing it out or presenting it as a PowerPoint presentation, he gave a sermon entitled *Game On*. He told everyone to wear a shirt or jersey from their favorite sports team. We had cracker jacks and popcorn during worship and we saw a movie clip from *Facing the Giants*. It's the scene where the student doesn't think he can do the drill but the coach blindfolds him and encourages him to do it anyway. The student makes it across the entire field (much further than he was told he'd go) and carries someone heavier than he thought.

The point of the message is that we can do what we put our mind to and often, even when we think we can't, God helps us do more than we think we can. So even though we were still a young church, and even though we'd accomplished a lot despite many odds against us, it was only the beginning. We had done so much but God was not finished with us yet. That day was the beginning of *game on* for Lighthouse. We were starting again with a new outlook and moving forward to get things done.

It was a major turning point for Lighthouse. We knew then that the training and hard work was worth it. We knew that possibilities were ahead of us and we were willing to work together to transform lives.

We began to think of where we were at the time and not where we came from. We began playing the game for real and running to win. Winning isn't everything, but when you can guarantee a win, you take it. Living for Jesus guarantees a win. Not a flat, easy course, but a win that will take us further than we can imagine.

You know that in a race all the runners run, but only one gets the prize. So run to win! All those who compete in the games use self-control so they can win a crown. That crown is an earthly thing that lasts only a short time, but our crown will never be destroyed.
—1 Corinthians 9:24-25, NCV

Chapter 13: Superheroes

The controlled chaos is one way to get creativity. The intensity of it, the physical rush, the intimacy created the kind of dialogue that leads to synergy.
—*Richard Holbrooke*

Mark has a gift that I'm not sure I'll ever possess—the ability to remember someone's name. Those of you with this gift often take it for granted but, for someone like me who really NEEDS this gift in her job, it is really horrible not to have it.

Names are important. They were important to God. Even the name of God was important in Biblical times. Moses asked, "Who should I say sent me?"

God replied "Tell them *I AM* sent you."

This is not really a name we can call God by, but more of a description of how we can think about God – always there.

Mark's idea of hospitality is amazing. Allan could work a room and dispense jobs like an employment agency. I can find a new friend and get many details about them and follow up with a personal touch. But Mark can tell you after meeting ten new people all of their names and at least one unique fact about them. This comes in handy the next time he sees them. Being called by name makes a person feel important. It shows you care and that you listened. I'm not a great listener. My ADD brain gets in the way of what someone is saying and what I'm having for lunch later. So for me to remember something other than how cute your shoes are is a LOT of work. Not for Mark. He's meant to make people feel at home. No matter why they show up or how long it's been, he makes people feel welcome.

Before we started Lighthouse there was a family on our launch team that I started getting to know. I had gotten to know the wife, Fonda, and had met her husband a few times. Fonda had even called me once at home and the Caller ID read what I thought was *Fonda and Brooks Totten*. So every time I met her husband I called him Brooks. I introduced him as Brooks. I had great conversations with

Brooks. It wasn't until one of our major planning meetings that I called Brooks by this name and everyone was confused. They asked, "You mean Bobby?"

You see, Fonda had hyphenated her name and Fonda Brooks-Totten was married to Bobby Totten. I felt like a HUGE idiot. How can someone be able to explain the doctrine of transubstantiation and not be able to remember *Bobby* who shares the same name as her father? Luckily, it didn't damage my relationship with the Tottens and we are able to laugh about it to this day.

Mark has a small obsession with superheroes. He loves to preach about them because they make great examples of Christian ideals. As the first year at Lighthouse progressed, many heroes emerged. Those people, I believe, saved my spiritual life during the year after Allan's death. These people were there for me when I cried, made me laugh when I needed to, and carried me when I just couldn't get up. And better yet, they did the same for total strangers all year long because of their love for God.

Superheroes aren't just stories made up to entertain people. Superheroes are real. Some people might call them angels. Others might call them saints, but whatever name you give them, they have special powers that I just don't possess. Lighthouse had more superheroes that most churches. Here are just a few:

- The Baby Whisperer – able to quiet any baby in just a single rocking motion
- The Laughing Mama – able to laugh out loud during sermons when others wouldn't have gotten the joke without hearing her
- The Carpenter – able to build VBS props no matter how absurd
- The Teenage Stupefier —able to confuse a teenager into doing something good and make them think it was his or her idea
- The Business Planner – able to make us focus on our business plan (to transform lives) without having us actually write down a detailed business plan with bullets that would probably get ignored anyway

- The Visitationator – able to know who needs a visit and when without being asked
- The Synergizer – able to take collective ideas and turn them into one unique and creative idea inspired by the Holy Spirit
- The Name Recaller – able to remember names and details at the drop of a hat

These superheroes may seem farcical but they are real people who can do things that I can't. They are using their spiritual gifts and applying them in ways that could only be attributed to God. Knowing them inspires me to be the person God calls me to be.

Perhaps we are all superheroes. Maybe our spiritual gifts make us superheroes when we use them for others and not for ourselves. For when I see the good in others, I see the good of Jesus – the greatest superhero ever!

A long time ago you spoke in a vision, you spoke to your faithful beloved: 'I've crowned a hero, I chose the best I could find'.
—Psalm 89:18, The Message.

Chapter 14: The Duck

The term *synergy* comes from the Greek word *synergia* συνεργία from *synergos*, συνεργός, meaning "working together".
—*The Strategy Reader, Edited by Susan Segal-Horn*

Everyone needs a nemesis. Perry has Dr. Doofenschmirtz. Road Runner has Coyote. Bugs Bunny has Elmer Fudd. Jesus has Satan.

Whether your nemesis is real or imaginary, it's great to have someone to blame when things go wrong. And even if they don't really do anything wrong, there's usually someone in your life that does some things that are laughable, and it's fun to know it's not you.

I love Disney movies. I always like the idea that the person that doesn't have everything going for them can end up becoming a prince or princess, taking an adventure on the East Australian Current, or returning home to save his *pride*. To me these stories have themes of the Gospel. There is always the least, the last and the lost who has to battle an enemy but because of the love and sacrifice of someone else, the hero can rise to the top (from last to first).

These seem like great movies to show to our children and, after a certain age, they are great lessons. Unfortunately, by the time someone is old enough to really understand the forces of good and evil portrayed in these movies, they have moved on and are *too old* to appreciate the genre until they are *older*.

The problem with showing these movies to young children is things seem cartoony and childish to us, but have some really scary parts for kids. The Little Mermaid seems like a sweet movie about a young girl and her funny fishy friends wanting adventure– to us. But to a four year old, Ursula is very, very scary. She's big (and gets bigger near the end) and ugly and pure evil.

We like to think that people aren't like this. We condition ourselves to see people as if they are Ariel and forget how scary Ursula can be. But there are some people that are just mean. Vicious. Evil. And we think that since the baby Jesus was all shining stars and singing angels, then church people should be angelic as well. Even those of us who have been burned by a mean church lady are honestly surprised when we run into a hypocrite in the church.

Of course, hypocrites are one thing. We all can be one at some point. But what really is destructive are the mean people who tip the balance into emotionally wounding. Pastors tend to be great targets for these nemeses. I don't know why these people come into our lives, but they are in every church. I was once told by a church consultant that if you are really doing God's work, the enemy will come at you strongly; but if you are just a caretaker of religious traditions, the enemy won't bother you. I guess at Lighthouse we were moving in the right direction.

I can't say that we had just one nemesis. There were several times that we had to deal with accusations you just can't make up. Mark and I personified these accusations into a comic book style character called *The Duck*.

It just made it easier to deal with knowing that The Duck was a bit *quackers* and it reminded us that in the end, we would win. The Duck was always putting us down. The Duck thought that we could do nothing right. The Duck always had a back story that only made sense to him or her. The Duck wanted to pull us down to his or her level so that we could experience his or her pain.

I know that it sounds awful that a pastor would jest about one of his or her flock. But The Duck was never really part of our flock. We wanted The Duck to be part of our flock, but The Duck would never buy into the vision. The Duck had other reasons to be at church than to follow Jesus. At first The Duck's actions seemed hurtful and mean, but then we saw that The Duck was just annoying. If The Duck really had been a hindrance, he or she would have ruined our spirit, but instead The Duck was about as effective as the Coyote, and gave us something to laugh about.

Ducks appear in every church. I've been told that I needed to tell parents how to dress their children before they come to church. I've been in a church meeting where someone brought his dogs. Large, menacing German shepherds. I was told once that my priorities weren't in order when my kid was sick and I stayed home to take care of him. Another time I was given a book on parenting *for use in my ministry* only to discover that it was published by the Jehovah's

Witnesses. I was accused of lying and altering a photo of our youth group because there was no way we had that many kids on a Sunday night. I could go on and on.

All different Ducks. It was great to finally give a name to this person. The Duck is different from Granola (fruits, flakes, and nuts) in that The Duck isn't just a little loopy. The Duck often veers over into the hurtful side of things. I am still not sure that the parenting book wasn't a jab at my parenting skills. It hurts me to think that someone would critique something so personal about me. As a pastor I know my life is more transparent than other's lives. But my hope is that, even when they judge me, they don't feel that I'm doing something so wrong in how I rear my children that I'll need a book to help me out.

Turning people like this into a cartoon nemesis makes me realize that if I really want to be a hero or at least follow a hero, I have to know that there are some people out there that will try and spoil my plans. In the end, they won't survive because they don't have the very thing that will help me succeed – a family of God.

"An enemy. An adversary. This evil Haman," said Esther. Haman was terror-stricken before the king and queen.
—Esther 7:6, The Message

Chapter 15: 'Ohana Means Family

In the long history of humankind (and animal kind, too) those who learned to collaborate and improvise most effectively have prevailed.
—Charles Darwin

In the movie Lilo and Stitch, Lilo says, "'Ohana means family, family means nobody gets left behind. Or forgotten."

The meaning of 'Ohana is more than just blood relation. It is a word that can be attributed to shared situations that bring people closer together.

One of the things that I've noticed little girls do is *play house*. They assign parts of the family – *you be the daddy, you be the mommy, you be the granny…* They assume that you know what each person in the family does (because you need to do what those people in that girl's family do.) Daddy works at Coca-Cola so he *makes Coke*. Mommy works at church so you'll need to read the Bible and pray if you have this role. Grandpa gets in trouble at restaurants so you need to hang spoons from your face and try to make people laugh.

Boys don't *play house*. They play *house building*. Forgive the gender stereotypes for just a minute, but boys tend to be more concerned with the location of the rooms, the right furniture, and props for family members to do their jobs, than who has what responsibility. They have a need to provide space and necessities that make a building realistic.

When I first got married, I was thrilled to be able to *play house* in real life. I had a husband and although we were renting, we had a real kitchen with real pots and pans and real food to cook. Setting a table for the two of us was fun, not a chore. On weekends, my husband and I visited open houses and dreamed big dreams of what our first house would look like. When I looked at these houses, I mentally arranged furniture and looked at what layout would be best for our future family. My husband looked at what would be a good investment, so that we'd be better off financially. But out of all those things, it wasn't until many years later that I finally felt like we had a home.

Little by little, I felt like we were becoming more home-worthy. We bought our first house. We had our first pets – two cats that were great starter pets. We had two boys (then the cats went crazy and ended up getting sick too often. They went to cat paradise way too early and I'm convinced they were jealous of the boys). We moved to a bigger house. We had a baby girl. Each one of these life events moved us closer to that feeling of home.

It never really felt like home to me until we got our dog, Roxy. We got Roxy from the pound. We thought we were getting a mostly grown black lab mix, but when we took her to the vet we were told that the dog was only four months old. Roxy was going to get BIG. Even before Roxy got big, she filled up the house. Even though she drove us crazy with house-training and obedience issues, we loved her instantly. The feeling that we gave a good home to a dog who otherwise would have been put to sleep, made us happy.

I'd like to say that Lighthouse was a family from the very beginning. In a sense it was. We met on Sundays. We broke bread in each other's homes. We prayed for each other. It wasn't just one particular event but a series of circumstances that helped us grow closer together. Even as people moved away or moved on from Lighthouse, the core people from our first year became family and were yoked together. The disciples had to do the same after Jesus died. We were able to hear the call just as clearly – to follow in their footsteps and spread the message.

But I'd have to say that one of the moments that made Lighthouse feel like home was when Mrs. Opal joined the church. Mrs. Opal had come to church with her daughter one Sunday. Mrs. Opal was in a wheelchair and had terminal cancer. Mrs. Opal was so moved by our church that she asked to be baptized (for the first time – Methodists do this only once). As I assisted in the baptism, I saw her face filled with a radiance I had previously only seen in teenagers who have discovered what God is all about. I teared up when her daughter laid hands on her mother knowing that one of the last acts of her mom's life would be life-changing.

Mrs. Opal died a few months later, but I'll never forget that baptism. We helped give Mrs. Opal a home she wouldn't have had otherwise. When you help to transform someone's life, you are connected to them eternally. I'm not just talking about giving Mrs. Opal a ticket to heaven. Yes heaven is important, but it is much, much more than that. We were there when Mrs. Opal experienced God, when she made a covenant with God, and when she began a new relationship with Him that would bring about more love and life in the world.

This was a celebration! Even though the time we knew Mrs. Opal was short and she's no longer in this world, she isn't left behind. She is still part of us and that small time we had together made her part of the family.

In a church family, no one gets left behind. Forget about dysfunctional families for a second. When someone in the family needs something, the other people are there for them. Lighthouse will always be that way. Even though I left Lighthouse in 2010, congregation members still pray for me, visit with me, break bread in my home, and always have my back.

Lighthouse is my ʻohana. My experience there will never be forgotten. It will always be a celebration.

The Spirit you received does not make you slaves, so that you live in fear again; rather, the Spirit you received brought about your adoption to sonship. And by him we cry, "Abba, Father."
—*Romans 8:15, NIV*

Chapter 16: Celebrations

We may have all come on different ships, but we are on the same boat now.
—*Martin Luther King Jr.*

As we celebrated the first birthday of Lighthouse, there were bittersweet moments. We never thought we'd be where we were at that time—still experiencing moments of grief, but healing was well on its way.

Normally a birthday is celebrated with friends, family, presents and cake. Talk to any four year old, and she will tell you that no birthday is complete without cake. Lighthouse was no exception. We had a HUGE cake with a lighthouse on it and one candle. Mark and I blew out the candle and posed for a picture with icing on our noses.

It seems weird to celebrate a 1st birthday of a church when The Church itself is almost 2000 years old. But just as each person is different within his or her family, each congregation is distinct from the larger, universal church. I tend to think of congregations as the children and denominations as family units. We don't always agree on how things should get done, but we generally agree on what things should get done and why.

There were so many things that I learned that first year. Here are the three big ones.

1) Never compromise the mission. I'm not sure why I like the Blues Brothers. Maybe it's because Jake and Elwood had cool suits and sunglasses. Maybe it's because there was some great music in the movie. Perhaps it is that I ended up loving Saturday Night Live characters and I was smart before my time. But I have to think that the fact that Jake and Elwood were on a *mission from God* has something to do with it. Their mission was to raise money to save the orphanage that raised them. They stayed with the mission until it was completed.

My mission is to equip others to make disciples to transform the world. The good news is that in many ways this is vague. The bad news is that in many ways this is vague. I see my part of the mission is to teach people about Jesus, then get them to apply his teaching and, therefore, change the world. Then those people are supposed to teach others about Jesus and get them to apply his teaching and transform the world even more. I guess in some ways it really is just a faith pyramid scheme. But there are so many other things such as new birth, Baptism and Communion and other big words like sanctification, justification, and prevenient grace that are all part of the *teaching about Jesus* and need to fit into the mission on a higher plane than *do not worry*.

These details are what make it easy to compromise the mission. When you want to teach Bible studies and others want to have more social outings because Jesus told us that fellowship is important, then you have a choice to make.

There were several times at Lighthouse where people wanted to compromise the mission. It was not that they wanted to go in a direction that was non-Christian or unethical. They just wanted to do something different from what the leadership wanted to do. We had one person who wanted to start a kid's handbell choir. I'm at a church now that has a kid's handbell choir. I love it. But at Lighthouse we weren't at that point yet and our target demographic wasn't receptive to that type of children's program. We had another person who thought we should be *recruiting* (her words) the rich people in the community so that we could better fund the programs we wanted to do. In some sense that person was thinking along the right lines. We do need money in order to do some of the things that will transform the world, but her idea took the focus away from God and onto the money or programs.

By staying on the mission, we transformed lives. We grew closer to God and to each other. We were able to overcome a tragic start and move people to a joyous future. We kept doing what we said we were going to do when we started. We may not have had as many dangerous adventures as Jake and Elwood, but we had lots of fun all the same.

2) Remember that life is short. We know this. But when we are reminded of this by mourning someone who died too soon, we tend to do things differently and look at the world differently.

After Allan died, I felt the need to increase life insurance on myself and my husband. I always had this task in the back of my mind but after August 2006, I couldn't rest until it was done. We also updated our wills and wrote down important stories for our kids. Things on the *To Do Someday* list suddenly moved up to the *ASAP* list.

I am one of those rare girls that doesn't really like to shop. I feel like the fashion designers are out to get me and that retail stores are contributing to the demise of a simpler life. While shopping, some women feel their mission in life is to get the best deal or buy the best fashions. My mission is to get in and out of the mall with my list checked off as soon as possible. I'm efficient. I spare no time for browsing.

I've always been a list maker. Checking things off my list is important to me. It just makes life easier. Many say that the problem with lists is that they leave no time for quiet or fun. I beg to differ. Fun and quiet are always bullet points on my list.

During the first year after Lighthouse started, my lists were still important to me. I still made them for shopping, for household to-dos, and ministry to-dos. But I noticed toward the end of the year I had more items like *enjoy lunch with Fonda* or *swim with the kids*. You may think that these items are small stuff, but to me they became priorities. Instead of looking at lunch with Fonda as a way to network, lunch with Fonda became about relationships. Swimming with the kids became less about wearing them out or getting exercise and more about making memories. I even think I took a few moments to browse when they were available to me.

When you realize that life is short, your to-do list becomes even shorter. The things that are important to you rise to the top and become your focus. I'm still a list maker and I still try to be as efficient as possible. I've learned that if my main focus remains
        1) God
        2) Family
        3) Friends
Then I'm being my best and most efficient.

3) Love makes all things new. Love is one of those exciting words that can be turned into any part of speech. It can mean happy things to some people, painful reminders to some, and a hopeful future to others. Our English word for love is inadequate for the myriad things it stands for. Other languages have different words for Godly love, passionate love, sacrificial love, and the love you have for bacon (okay I may have made that last one up but that kind of love really should have its own word!)

When I was young, I thought love was something that your parents were legally obligated to tell you and also something reserved for people who were going to get married. These beliefs would have kept things simple. It would have meant that parents did tell their kids that they loved them. Instead I came to realize that not all parents love their children and others do not show it. We should not throw the word *love* around as if it were a Frisbee. It should be a word reserved for those who believe in forever.

It is hard to imagine a world without love. I've lived in a bubble all of my life. At first this bubble was placed around me by my family. Since then, for the most part, my bubble has been self-imposed. The great thing about bubbles is that you can see out of them, but even though you know what is going on outside of the bubble, the climate is so different, you can't really comprehend what it is like until you venture out. Although I haven't always wanted to, I have left my bubble at times. I've seen how other people live and tried to help. I've tried to share what I have. I try to share God's love.

I share God's love because I know that God has made a difference in my life. Despite my bubble, I have been able to experience the joy that comes from God's love. I understand the healing that God's love offers when one has lost the love of a friend. There were moments during Lighthouse's first year that I felt God wiping away my tears. I felt a new heaven and a new earth being made and I knew that because of God's love and the love shown to me by my church family, everything would be okay. In fact it would be more than okay, I would never be alone.

Then I saw "a new heaven and a new earth," for the first heaven and the first earth had passed away, and there was no longer any sea, I saw the Holy City, the new Jerusalem, coming down out of heaven from God, prepared as a bride beautifully dressed for her husband. And I heard a loud voice from the throne saying, "Look! God's dwelling place is now among the people, and he will dwell with

them. They will be his people, and God himself will be with them and be their God. 'He will wipe every tear from their eyes. There will be no more death' or mourning or crying or pain, for the old order of things has passed away." He who was seated on the throne said, "I am making everything new!" Then he said, "Write this down, for these words are trustworthy and true."
—Revelation 21:1-5, NIV

Notes

Chapter One
This Is Your Time by Michael W. Smith (©) 2004 Reunion Records

Chapter Two
SIX FLAGS and all related indicia, symbols and designs are trademarks and/or the subject of copyrights of Six Flags Theme Parks Inc. ®, TM and ©.
"Physics of Roller Coasters." *Wikipedia*. Wikimedia Foundation, 29 May 2012. Web. 10 June 2012.
http://en.wikipedia.org/wiki/Physics_of_roller_coasters
"Infinite Loop." *Wikipedia*. Wikimedia Foundation, 06 Oct. 2012. Web. 10 June 2012. http://en.wikipedia.org/wiki/Infinite_loop

Chapter Three
Chick-fil-A® is a registered trademark of CFA Properties, Inc. ("CFA Properties"), is licensed to Chick-fil-A, Inc., and is registered in the United States and other countries.
©2011 WH Capital, L.L.C. ®™ All Waffle House trademarks are owned by WH Capital, L.L.C. and licensed to Waffle House, Inc.
© 2012 The Ritz-Carlton Hotel Company, L.L.C. All rights reserved.

Chapter Four
Seinfeld is a product of © 1990–1998 Castle Rock Entertainment. All Rights Reserved. And © 2012 Sony Pictures Digital Inc. All Rights Reserved.

Chapter Five
AT&T, the AT&T logo, AT&T slogans and other AT&T product/service names and logos are trademarks and service marks of AT&T Intellectual Property or AT&T affiliated company ("AT&T Marks").

Chapter Six
Seinfeld is a product of © 1990–1998 Castle Rock Entertainment. All

Rights Reserved. And © 2012 Sony Pictures Digital Inc. All Rights Reserved.

Chapter Seven
Walt Disney World® Resort in Florida

Chapter Eight
Avalanche Ranch, Group and "Group Publishing Materials", are owned by or licensed to Group Publishing.

Chapter Nine
IKEA © Inter IKEA Systems B.V. 1999–2011
PEZ© Copyright 2010 PEZ Candy Inc, USA. All rights reserved.
LOONEY TUNES and all related characters and elements are trademarks of and © Warner Bros. Entertainment Inc.
BATMAN, SUPERMAN, JUSTICE LEAGUE and all related characters and elements are trademarks of and© DC Comics.
Staples and Easy Button Copyright 2011, Staples, Inc., All Rights Reserved.
Rubik® and Rubik's Cube® are registered trademarks throughout the world of Seven Towns Limited.
Barbie © 2012 Mattel, Inc. All Rights Reserved.
Where's Waldo © 2009 Classic Media Distribution Ltd. All rights reserved.

Chapter Ten
Magna Doodle Fischer Price
©2012 Mattel, Inc. All Rights Reserved.

Chapter Twelve
Facing the Giants ©2006 Sherwood Baptist Church Albany, GA Inc.

Chapter Fifteen
Lilo and Stitch Disney Enterprises, Inc. Walt Disney Television Animation
© 2011 The Coca-Cola Company, all rights reserved.

Study Guide for Group Discussions

Chapter One: For Such A Time As This
- What are some of the most memorable events of your faith journey?
- In what ways did you participate in those events, and how did they change your point of view toward the future?
- How do you think God prepared you for each of those events?
- When you think about the death of a close friend or family member, how do you honor that person?
- Have you ever worked with someone so closely that you could almost read their mind?
- How do you try to create synergy when brainstorming ministry ideas?

Chapter Two: Roller Coaster
- What is the scariest thing you've ever done?
- Do you tend to stay away from risk or embrace it?
- What steps do you take in planning events?
- When God calls you to do something, do you need to come up with a Plan B?

Chapter Three: Weird-Ass Issues
- What are your personal quirks that make you unique?
- How are you able to work with others that don't share these differences with you?
- Are your issues something that make you a unique child of God or something that you need God's help with in order to overcome them?

Chapter Four: The Big Ask
- What is the most outrageous thing that anyone has ever asked you to do?
- What makes the difference in you accepting or declining a new responsibility?

Chapter Five: Organizational Systems
- What organizational style do you adhere to?

- Can you name one or two tools for organizing that you cannot do without?
- What role does prayer play in your organizational process?

Chapter Six: Unbalanced
- What is the oddest task you've ever done in a job that wasn't part of the job description?
- Do you get a sense of accomplishment from completing a task?
- How can you get a sense of accomplishment from on-going ministries that have no clear start or stop date?

Chapter Seven: Drugs and Disney
- Is there a place that you can go to in order to get away or recharge yourself after a time of stress?
- Has that place ever failed you? If so, why?
- Can you recognize the signs of depression in others and do you know the best ways to offer them help?

Chapter Eight: Saying Goodbye
- What is the most memorable way that someone has ever said good-bye to you?
- Why is it important to say good-bye to someone who has passed away?
- How do you know when you've achieved a sense of closure?

Chapter Nine: First Impressions
- What is the worst first impression you've ever gotten from a restaurant?
- Did that restaurant ever redeem the impression you had? If so, what did it take to change your opinion?
- When you have a great first impression, how do you respond?
- Why are first impressions so important to the Kingdom of God?

Chapter Ten: Answering Your Own Questions
- Why are we so reluctant to answer questions in public? (fear of being wrong)

- How can someone make you feel more comfortable in sharing your ideas? (share his or her ideas first perhaps?)
- What are some interesting ways that people communicate that help you remember the message? (answering his or her own questions, repeating a catch phrase, using a jingle, or using a vivid example)

Chapter Eleven: The Holy Spirit: A Hostage Situation
- How do you handle conflict in your family?
- What role does the Holy Spirit play in family conflicts?

Chapter Twelve: Game On!
- When do you know when you are ready to compete for something?
- Once you launch a big project, what are the signs that it has moved from the planning stage to the up-and-running stage?

Chapter Thirteen: Superheroes
- Who are the heroes in your life?
- What are some of the characteristics of un-sung heroes that you know?

Chapter Fourteen: The Duck
- Who or what is the nemesis in your life?
- How do you think that God views that person?
- What can you do to see that person the way that God does?

Chapter Fifteen: 'Ohana Means Family
- Have you ever been left behind or physically lost somewhere?
- What would it feel like to know that you'll never be left behind?
- Who are the people in your life that are your 'ohana?

Chapter Sixteen: Celebrations
- What are your favorite ways to celebrate?
- How can you evaluate a successful event so that you see the growing edges but so that you are still able to enjoy the celebration?

Still reading???

Just as no one does ministry alone, no one writes a book alone. If I haven't said thank you, then my mom and grandmother will find me and shame me. There are too many people to name here but since this book is about gratitude please know that I am grateful for everyone who has helped me along the way including my family, congregation members, proof-readers, and shoulders to cry on.

Thanks.

About the Author

Rev. Shannon Karafanda is an Ordained Deacon in the United Methodist Church with a focus on family ministries. She grew up in Morrow, Georgia, went to school at Georgia Tech, and worked as a computer programmer before pursuing her call to ministry in 1999. Oddly enough, she's discovered that programming and ministry are very similar. They both deal with people looking for answers, for new users the design is often just as important at the content, and change is difficult in either situation.

She went to Candler School of Theology and has worked in Family Ministries at Brooks UMC, Turin UMC, Lighthouse UMC, Sacred Tapestry, The Church at the Well, and Hopewell UMC; three of these were new church starts in the North Georgia Conference.

Shannon lives with he-who-shall-not-be-named-in-sermons (her husband), her three children and overly affectionate black lab in Peachtree City, GA. She is currently working part-time as a Youth Pastor. So she spends half her time figuring out how toilet paper can be used in a game that effectively communicates the Gospel and she spends the rest of her days ignoring the mess her kids have made, deciding if she should put on actual clothes vs. her pjs, and checking Facebook constantly just to prove to herself that most people aren't that exciting either.

When she's not on Facebook, you can find her on Twitter, blogging, reading books that no one would expect a minister to read, painting and running (usually not all at the same time).

For more or to contact Shannon, go to her website at www.UntilEveryoneHears.com.

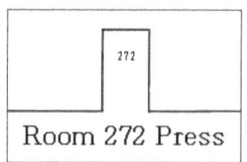

Room 272 Press is pleased to offer services to writers of fine books and their readers. Find out more about our other books and how we provide new authors assistance with access to the world of professional publication. We can help you make your dream a reality. www.Room272.weebly.com

Room 272 Press is an imprint of David Anders Publishing House. The occupants of Room 272 in Reed Hall at the University of Georgia were sometimes rowdy but always well intentioned, as chronicled in the romantic comedy *20/80 A Love Letter...Sort Of*. Visit us at www.AndersUSA.com to learn more about our books, our authors, and how to enjoy both.

www.ingramcontent.com/pod-product-compliance
Lightning Source LLC
LaVergne TN
LVHW051847080426
835512LV00018B/3119

9780615653532